Marginal Cost
in the New Economy

Marginal Cost
in the New Economy

A Proposal
for a Uniform
Approach
to Policy
Evaluations

Roger L. Conkling

M.E.Sharpe
Armonk, New York
London, England

Material has been quoted from the following sources with permission:

Bergson, Abram, "Socialist Economics," in *A Survey of Contemporary Economics*, ed., Howard S. Ellis (New York: McGraw-Hill Education, 1949). Reprinted with permission from the McGraw-Hill Education, a Division of The McGraw-Hill Companies.

Bonbright, James C., *Principles of Public Utility Rates* (New York: Columbia University Press, 1961). Reprinted with permission from Columbia University Press, New York.

Bork, Robert H., *The Antitrust Paradox: A Policy at War with Itself* (New York: Basic Books, 1978). Reprinted with permission from Perseus Books Group, New York.

Kahn, Alfred E., "Application of Economics to an Imperfect World," *American Economic Review* 69, no. 2 (Nov./Dec. 1978). Reprinted with permission from the American Economic Association, Nashville, TN.

_____, "Application of Economics to Utility Rate Structures," *Public Utilities Fortnightly*, Jan. 19, 1978. Reprinted with permission from Public Utilities Reports, Vienna, VA.

_____, "Can an Economist Find Happiness Setting Public Utility Rates?" *Public Utilities Fortnightly*, Jan. 5, 1978. Reprinted with permission from Public Utilities Reports, Vienna, VA.

_____, "Can Regulation and Competition ..." *The Electricity Journal* (1994). Reprinted with permission from Elsevier Science, Oxford UK.

_____, *The Economics of Regulation*. Reprinted with permission from the author.

_____, "The Economics of Regulation: Externalities and Institutional Issues," *Public Utilities Fortnightly*, Feb. 2, 1978. Reprinted with permission from Public Utilities Reports, Vienna, VA.

_____, "Electric Deregulation ..." *The Electricity Journal* 11, no. 3 (1998): 39–49. Reprinted with permission from Elsevier Science, Oxford UK.

_____, *Letting Go* (Easting Lansing, MI: Institute of Public Utilities, MSU, 1998). Reprinted with permission from Michigan State University, East Lansing, MI.

Kahn, Alfred E., and William B. Shew, "Current Issues in Telecommunications Regulation: Pricing," *The Yale Journal on Regulation* (Spring 1987). Reprinted with permission from Yale Law School, New Haven, CT.

Pearce, David W., ed., *The MIT Dictionary of Modern Economics*, 4th ed. (Cambridge, MA: The MIT Press, 1992). Reprinted with permission from The MIT Press, Cambridge, MA.

Ruggles, Nancy, "Developments in the Theory of Marginal Cost Pricing," *The Review of Economic Studies* 17 (1949–1950). Reprinted with permission from the Review of Economic Studies, Bath, UK.

Library of Congress Cataloging-in-Publication Data

Conkling, Roger L., 1917–
    Marginal cost in the new economy: a proposal for a uniform approach to policy evaluations / Roger L. Conkling.
        p. cm.
    Includes bibliographical references.
    ISBN 0-7656-0849-9 (alk. paper)
    1. Direct costing. 2. Policy sciences. I. Title.

HF5686.C8C6732 2004
338.5′1—dc22

2003061406

Printed in the United States of America

The paper used in this publication meets the minimum requirements of American National Standard for Information Sciences Permanence of Paper for Printed Library Materials, ANSI Z 39.48-1984.

BM (c) 10   9   8   7   6   5   4   3   2   1

This book is dedicated to Alfred E. Kahn
scholar, educator, and government executive
who inspired recognition and application
of marginal cost principles

Contents

Acknowledgments

My gratitude to the University of Portland (UP) knows no bounds. The University undertook to sponsor this book (including a possible second volume, *The Great Micro Price Experiment*) as a venture with results unknown, and has done all draft typing, retyping, printing, and reprinting, without question as to substance or lack thereof. I am particularly grateful to Brother Donald J. Stabrowski, C.S.C., Provost, for his support and encouragement.

I am also grateful to several other University members for their painstaking transcriptions of this manuscript from almost illegible handwritten drafts to final copy: Sharon Rossmiller, in the early stages, and Gwynn Klobes with Tracy Peterson (a most promising student) in the later stages. Only someone lacking computer skills could grasp my appreciation of Sharon, Gwynn, and Tracy.

My gratitude extends also to Angela Doescher, who conformed the manuscript to the format of the publisher, while at the same time struggling to segregate the present volume from its possible successor, and to Linda Cady, at UP, who printed the manuscript from various disassociated disks. Further, I thank Lynn Taylor, Executive Editor, Economics, M.E. Sharpe, Inc. for her patience in guiding the manuscript through the labyrinth of the publication process.

Finally, I thank Alfred E. Kahn for permission to quote from his famous book, *The Economics of Regulation*; and I am grateful to Judge Diarmuid F. O'Scannlain for his review of chapter 7.

Roger L. Conkling

Introduction
The Policy Clash

Marginal Cost Pricing is beneficial, because it results in economic efficiency.

Marginal Cost Pricing is detrimental, because it discourages new investment.

Which is right as a guide for the New Economy?

Each of these pricing guidelines is at least partially correct. Each has economic merit. But, placed side by side, they clash, predisposing of each other. Public policies based on one are unavoidably in conflict with policies based on its opposite. Neither guide can be accepted on its face as the Golden Rule for costing and pricing in the New Economy. Nor can either be rejected outright.

Each guideline has a place in directing the twenty-first-century economy. The dilemma lies in determining the circumstances that make it appropriate to choose one guide or the other.

The policy relevance of the first guideline, the traditional holding that marginal cost pricing is a desideratum from the standpoint of efficiency, must be weighted in the light of the emergence of the New Economy, with its demands that prices be sufficient to finance at least the costs of innovation in addition to marginal costs.

Marginal Cost Pricing = Economic Efficiency

Neoclassical microeconomics has long cherished the goal of structuring the economy so as to result in the most productive allocation of society's limited resources: in short, to enhance economic efficiency. The chosen path toward this goal is to price goods and services at their marginal cost of production.

In the traditional short-run marginal cost (SRMC) view, these costs comprise only the incremental changes in total costs that occur because of changes in output of physical plant (or infrastructure for a service industry) already in place. Because existing plant (or existing infrastructure) remains constant (although patterns of operations may shift), plant investment and infrastructure costs, together with other fixed costs not variable with output, are excluded from SRMC. These are considered to be "sunk" costs and are disregarded. In other words, short-run marginal costs include only variable costs that are incremental to a change in output.

This is the strict "first best" normative conclusion as to the efficient relationship of cost and price: Short-Run Marginal Cost = Price = Economic (Allocative) Efficiency.

Marginal Cost Pricing = Barrier to Investment

On May 10, 2000, former treasury secretary Lawrence Summers (now president of Harvard University) challenged the acceptance of SRMC as an economic guideline.[1] He saw the New Economy as demanding rapid innovation if its promise was to be realized. Innovation requires an inflow of new investment capital, particularly for research and development (R&D). Any yardstick that fails to include the recovery of investment costs in price is a deterrent, running counter to the need for continued infusions of capital. Even an implied suggestion of nonrecovery (such as the contention that competitive prices will eventually be bid down to marginal costs) is harmful.

So as not to deter innovation, Summers suggests that a temporary monopoly should be permitted to allow the innovative firm a near-guaranteed opportunity to recover its invested capital.

Antitrust

Since 1890, the nation has had antitrust laws in place that aim at protecting the economy from obstacles to its effective operation. The chosen path is the enhancement of competition by the prevention of monopoly and its abuses. The unstated objective of antitrust is to seek prices for consumers that would be as low as reasonably practicable.

The Policy Clash

Clearly, Summers's suggestion is at odds with both the normative goal of pricing at bare marginal cost to attain economic efficiency and the parallel antitrust goal of promoting competition to keep consumer prices low. A protected monopoly will set its prices higher than they would be under unfettered competition—in fact, that is its intent.

This is not to conclude, however, that the conflicting policies could not be in force harmoniously, side by side. None of the positions are absolute. They could coexist. It is recognized that the yardstick, Short-Run Marginal Cost = Price, precludes long-run viability for the impacted firm. Recovery *of*, and a return *on*, capital is essential for continuity of operations of any firm. The antitrust laws themselves permit patents and copyrights that are temporary monopolies granting price protection. There is no obvious reason why such price protection might not be extended to promote an additional policy objective, such as innovation, if policymakers decide to do so.

This Book: A Preview

As its central theme, this book proposes that marginal cost methodology be adopted as an economically sound uniform approach to many current and emerging public policy issues, thereby gaining consistency in evaluating cost-linked and price-linked questions. It also proposes that this same methodology could be a useful tool in the private sector, for corporations and other nongovernmental interest groups. These groups could adopt it as a uniform yardstick in evaluation of alternative courses of action to produce the same consistency in approach and results.

But uniformity and consistency in cost-price determinations are not achieved easily even using marginal cost techniques. Among the difficulties is the conflict between purist microeconomic price theory and the realities of the New Economy, referred to earlier as the policy clash. Chapters 1 and 2 explore this conflict from a middle-ground point of view. They point out the policy implications of dealing with industries, prevalent in the New Economy, which are characterized by high fixed costs and low marginal costs.

Chapter 1, "The Challenge to Orthodoxy," reports on a challenge to prevailing economics issued by a high government official, treasury secretary Lawrence Summers, in May 2000. Summers casts doubt upon the wisdom in the New Economy of a rigid interpretation of the antitrust laws, which pursue a marginal cost price as their end result. He suggests that a temporary monopoly for innovative firms might be required, so that their prices would not be bid down to marginal cost, and therefore fail to cover fixed costs.

Chapter 2, "Reflections on the Summers Thesis," examines the challenge from several points of view, beginning with a discussion of the short-run and long-run versions of marginal cost found in the literature, particularly as they affect the recovery of sunk costs. It includes consideration of whether capital inflows are induced by the profits anticipated to be included in future prices, the traditional view, or, as in the case of new capital pouring into cyberspace ventures, by speculative hope of stock-price appreciation. Economic fundamentals are also examined, such as whether the ingenuity of the mind, the fountain of the Information Age, is as limited as are the physical resources assumed by contemporary theory.

These first two chapters establish the requirement that a uniform method be sufficiently flexible to accommodate both conventional microeconomics and the expanded character of the New Economy.

Chapter 3, "Marginal Costs and Marginalism: Background and Application," outlines the principles of such a flexible method. It also lists the steps to be followed in a base-type evaluation study, leaving until later modifications in the base steps that are needed to mesh with the unique characteristics of the New Economy (such as situations requiring a specific recognition of innovation, including R&D, as a cost). The base steps are suited for the analysis of many public policy issues, but not all. Additional steps are needed for others.

Chapter 3 touches upon the principles to be kept in mind in making an evaluation of cost-price-linked issues using marginal cost methodology. In proposing that marginal costs be the starting point, it thus introduces textbook microeconomics, which is *normative* in nature. The role of marginal costs in prevailing economic thought cannot be fully appreciated unless the *normative* position is understood.

For perspective, it is important to distinguish between *positive* and *normative* economics.[2] *Positive* economics contends that under perfect competition prices will fall to marginal cost. Positive theory also points out that prices will not necessarily fall to marginal cost under monopolistic (or imperfect) competition, which actually dominates the U.S. economy— *not* perfect competition. These are conclusions of fact, without judgment as to whether the facts are good or bad, beneficial or detrimental.

The *normative* position posits that "prices *should* be set at marginal cost so as to attain economic efficiency," a position sometimes referred to as the "marginal cost pricing doctrine" (or simply "the doctrine"), to distinguish it from the analytical conclusion that prices *are* set at marginal cost under perfect competition.

Chapter 4, "Achieving Economic Efficiency in Regulated Pricing," lays out the normative logic—the foundation of the marginal cost pricing doctrine—as explained by its most influential protagonist, Alfred E. Kahn, in his two-volume book, *The Economics of Regulation*. Kahn notes the problems of defining marginal cost (short-run, long-run, or intermediate-run). He is fully aware that the conditions of perfect competition are not found in the actual economy, and explains why the doctrine is applicable nonetheless. Parallels to the Summers issue are easy to find despite the fact that when Kahn departs from pure theory, his specific references are to the utility industries (particularly electric). A little imagination will ease the transition from utilities to computer software, or fiber optics, or drugs, or whichever, as the individual reader may seek to apply the doctrine to his or her industry of interest.

For the most part, chapter 4 lets Kahn speak for himself by quoting him directly. The few comments that are interspersed are explanatory only.

Chapter 4 is supplemented by an appendix, "Pre–Kahn Theory," which is presented primarily for the microeconomist. It covers pricing theory as it stood prior to Kahn's *Economics*, comprising a good deal of the theoretic foundation available to him in constructing his thesis. The relevant contributions of four early writers are outlined: Abram Bergson on "Socialist Economics"; Abba P. Lerner, from the *Economics of Control: Principles of Welfare Economics*; Nancy Ruggles, on "Recent Developments in the Theory of Marginal Cost Pricing"; and James C. Bonbright, from *Principles of Public Utility Rates*. This appendix should be a convenient reference to the thoughts of these economists.

The next three chapters discuss the application of marginal cost methodology to public policy in the New Economy.

Chapter 5, "School Vouchers," illustrates the application of the base methodology to the school voucher issue.

The actual budget of a public school system is adopted to provide a factual basis for the study. The chapter shows the derivation from the budget of short-run and intermediate-run marginal costs (SRMC and IRMC, respectively), to approximate the amount of the school voucher allowance that might be offered for either time frame, and the financial effect of such vouchers upon the school from which students are transferred, assuming that voucher payments are deducted from the funds available to the school.

Chapter 6, "Special Cases: Mixed Issues/Mixed Methodologies," recognizes the variety of public policy issues for which the base methodology is inadequate.

Looming as particularly important in the New Economy are activities in such areas as prescription drugs that require large speculative investments in research. While drugs are a good example, and software another, the necessity for research extends into almost all activities in the Information Age from which innovation is desired. Research is treated as a special case, and expenditures for that function are included in the analysis, with particular attention to risk. Drug patent extensions are covered as a subset of the research issue.

Quasi-regulatory issues are another area of current interest. Questions may range from the simple cost/price effect of an incremental change in output (for which the base methodology probably suffices) to the complexities of evaluating a merger (requiring special case treatment).

This chapter concludes that direct price controls are inherently unworkable for prescription drugs and similar products that are not natural monopolies. However, the special cases suggest blueprints for a more limited surveillance of prices should that be deemed desirable.

Chapter 7, "Antitrust," briefly surveys the antitrust statutes. This survey is not a legal analysis. It covers only aspects of the antitrust laws that are relevant to marginal costs, or related to general economic theory. Then it describes marginal cost methodologies that could be enlisted to resolve traditional antitrust questions, such as: whether suspected collusion has raised a suspect price higher than would be justified by cost increases; whether suspected predatory pricing is indicated by a suspect price that is out-of-line with industry standards; and whether monopoly conditions are reflected in the price of the suspect monopolist. The chapter also examines the manner in which marginal cost methodology might be employed if innovation were to be adopted as an antitrust goal in parallel with the present goal of competition. A middle-ground approach is hypothesized, which might encourage innovation without necessitating a major change in the antitrust statutes.

Chapter 8 offers some "Concluding Thoughts."

* * *

Invariably, a policy change, or the extension of an existing policy to a new situation, gives rise to debate. Each side will argue at length in support of its view. But the ultimate question, almost always, is, what will the change cost? Cost estimates will vary widely because they will have different starting points and employ inconsistent methodologies. This results in public confusion and a clouding of facts.

To minimize the confusion, this book suggests that a common starting point—marginal cost, and a uniform methodology, marginalism— be substituted for the potpourri of approaches to cost determination that now dominate in discussions of policy issues.

Marginal cost has a solid position in economics, and marginalism bridges the gap between guidelines geared to the Old Economy and the revised guidelines required to meet the exigencies of the New Economy.

Marginal Cost
in the New Economy

1. The Challenge to Orthodoxy

The Boisterous Sea of Liberty is never without a wave.
—Thomas Jefferson

Introduction

"The Challenge to Orthodoxy" was launched by Lawrence H. Summers as secretary of the treasury, prior to his presidency of Harvard University. The challenge was laid down in skeletal fashion in a speech of May 10, 2000, on "The New Wealth of Nations."[1]

Various theoretical and practical issues implied in the challenge were later amplified and more fully explained in a paper by Summers as president of Harvard, written jointly with J. Bradford DeLong, professor at the University of California, Berkeley, and National Bureau of Economic Research (NBER), on a related subject, "The 'New Economy': Background, Historical Perspective, Questions, and Speculations."[2]

The joint paper does not directly repeat the challenge, and covers more ground than is included in Summers's 2000 speech. But it richly compliments the speech, and fills in the economic gaps therein. Chapters 1 and 2 quote extensively from these sources.

Because competition is the cornerstone of the nation's antitrust statutes, any change that would limit competition, whether statutory or interpretive, is likely to be the subject of heated debate. Chapters 1 and 2 provide some of the grist for that debate.

The New Economy

The New Economy is not yet defined in the economic literature,[3] but one fact is undeniable. The New Economy is different. Then-treasury secretary Lawrence H. Summers, in a May 10, 2000, speech, described it as "the move from an economy based on the production of physical goods to an economy based on the production and application of knowledge." The enhancement of knowledge will involve very large fixed costs and much smaller marginal (variable) costs.

The joint DeLong-Summers paper enlarges on that description, comparing the new economy to the old.

> We used to live in an economy in which the canonical source of value was an ingot of iron, a barrel of oil or a bushel of wheat. Such economies were based on knowledge just as much as our economy is, but the knowledge was of how to create a useful, physically-embodied good. We are moving to an economy in which the canonical source of value is a gene sequence, a line of computer code, or a logo. . . . In such an economy, what you know matters more than how much you can lift.

The joint paper also addresses the implications and some of the uncertainties of the shift to the new economy.

> The principal effects of the "new economy" are more likely to be "microeconomic" than "macroeconomic," and they will lead to profound—if at present unclear—changes in how the government should act to provide the property rights, institutional frameworks, and "rules of the game" that underpin the market economy.

> * * *

> The balance of probabilities is that our modern data processing and data communications technologies are indeed creating a "new economy." It is likely that they are producing profound change with continuing powerful impact. These are seismic innovations, ranking with electric power. Even if they are not likely to have profound impact in reducing cyclical volatility, they will have profound microeconomic effects that we do not yet fully understand. We already know that the competitive paradigm is unlikely to be fully appropriate, but we do not yet know what the right replacement paradigm will be. We know that property rights become a central question. We know that some market practices—such as price discrimination—that have traditionally been looked at with some skepticism should perhaps be reevaluated.

* * *

. . . the structural changes that we call the "new economy" are ongoing. Moreover, as the economy's structure changes, desirable government policies change as well. If we step back a bit, we can see that the governmental foundations underpinning the market system necessary to make it function well are not fixed in stone. As technology and society have changed in the past, what the government needed to do in order to make the market function changed too.

* * *

. . . in the "new economy" more markets will be contestable. Competitive edges based on past reputations or brand loyalty or advertising footprints will fade away. As they do so, profit margins will fall: competition will become swifter, stronger, more pervasive, and more nearly perfect.

Consumers will gain and shareholders will lose. Those products that can be competitively supplied will be at very low margins. The future of the technology is bright; the future of the profit margins of businesses—save for those few that truly are able to use economies of scale to create mammoth cost advantages—is dim.

* * *

. . . our modern computer and communication technologies simply make it too cheap and too easy to distribute a competing product.

The Challenge to Orthodoxy

Taking up the large fixed-to-smaller variable cost relationships that he saw would accompany the enhancement of knowledge in the New Economy, Summers in his 2000 speech launched a direct challenge to orthodox microeconomics, on the one hand, and to orthodox antitrust precepts, on the other. Instead of deploring all monopoly and lauding marginal cost pricing, keynotes of widely accepted prevailing doctrines, he advocated a reverse. For the New Economy, he declared: *"The only incentive to produce anything is the possession of temporary monopoly power—because without that power the price will be bid down to marginal cost and the high initial fixed costs cannot be recouped.* So the constant pursuit of that monopoly power becomes the central driving thrust of the new economy. And the creative destruction that results from all that striving becomes the essential spur of economic growth. In that sense, if the agricultural economies were Smithian[4] the new economy is Schumpeterian"[5] (emphasis added).

The 2001 joint paper explains the Smithian-to-Schumpeterian analogy, concluding that the competitive Smithian paradigm fits the old economy but fails to be fully appropriate for the new. It states:

> . . . if we call the economy of the past two centuries primarily "Smithian," the economy of the future is likely to be primarily "Schumpeterian." In a "Smithian" economy, the decentralized market economy does a magnificent job (if the intial distribution of wealth is satisfactory) at producing economic welfare. Because goods are "rival"—my sleeping in this hotel bed tonight keeps you from doing so—one person's use or consumption imposes a social cost: Because good economic systems align the incentives facing individuals with the effects of their actions on social welfare, it makes sense to distribute goods by charging prices equal to marginal social cost. . . .
>
> The competitive paradigm is appropriate as a framework to think about issues of microeconomic policy and regulation.
>
> In a "Schumpeterian" economy, the decentralized economy does a much less good job. Goods are produced under conditions of substantial increasing returns to scale. This means that competitive equilibrium is not a likely outcome: the canonical situation is more likely to be one of natural monopoly. But natural monopoly does not meet the most basic condition for economic efficiency: that price equal marginal cost. However, forcing prices to be equal to marginal cost cannot be sustained because then the fixed set-up costs are not covered. Relying on government subsidies to cover fixed set-up costs raises problems of its own: it destroys the entrepreneurial energy of the market and replaces it with the group-think and red-tape defects of administrative bureaucracy. Moreover, in a Schumpeterian economy, it is innovation that is the principal source of wealth—and temporary monopoly power and profits are the reward needed to spur private enterprise to engage in such innovation. The right way to think about this complex set of issues is not clear, but it is clear that the competitive paradigm cannot be fully appropriate.

The Challenge Dissected

Both the antitrust statutes and prevailing economic thought treat monopoly as an evil, as a condition either to be eliminated or, if it is a "natural" monopoly, to be allowed to exist only under stringent price regulation.

The antitrust laws emphasize the advantages of untrammeled competition. Economics explains the reason, contending that prices will be higher and output lower under monopoly conditions than under competition, both of which are anathema to economic efficiency.

The first element of Summers's challenge is his refusal to accept the prevailing view that monopoly, simply by reason of its existence, should not be tolerated under any circumstances.[6]

Second, he goes further. He states flatly that a temporary monopoly[7] is necessary and essential to provide prices high enough to serve as an incentive for investment in a situation where initial costs are high but costs of production of the final product are low.

This situation of high initial and low production costs seem to be increasingly typical in an information economy. Certainly it is already widespread. High profile cases, such as Microsoft now pending in the courts, and the enormous public attention being given to the high prices of prescription drugs, are two illustrations of this cost phenomenon. For both software and new drugs, heavy expenditures for research and development (R&D) are required to engineer a final product. But when the final product is ready for market, production costs in total and per unit are miniscule. Thus a price that would recoup all costs would consist primarily of R&D recovery, with only a small portion for actual production.

The joint DeLong-Summers paper adds the following observations:

> High initial fixed costs and low, even zero marginal costs pose difficult questions but also open up enormous opportunities for economic policy. In a "new economy," the canonical industrial structure will be more like what we have seen in pharmaceuticals, publishing, or the recording industry than in the corn-production or textile or steel industry. The opportunity is that growth should have a greater potential to snowball. Success may have greater potential to become self-perpetuating, as growth leads to rapid declines in prices, and so to further expansion in the market and further growth. We see aspects of this today: orphan drugs cost much more than drugs with a larger market, and best selling books cost much less than academic monographs that very few people may read.
>
> This reality points up the importance of making sure that we function with as large markets as possible. When a market is driven by a positive feedback, its efficiency will be directly related to its size. Larger networks and larger production lines over which to amortize high initial fixed costs will generate cascading benefits. Thus government policies

that expand the size of markets in any way—through reducing trade barriers, through improved infrastructure, through the removal of other barriers to market access—become that much more important and that much more worthwhile.

As pointed out in the above quotation, Summers's second challenge to orthodoxy has widespread implications. The actual impact is unknown, of course, as of this writing, but the fact that a high government official sees some virtue in monopoly, even though the virtue is limited to specific circumstances, may set in motion an ever-widening ripple effect.

The third element of the challenge invokes economic theory as justification for the position that monopoly, in some circumstances at least, is in the public interest.

The linchpin of the argument is that absent monopoly power, that is, under effective competition, prices will sink to an aggressively competitive level. This level, according to generalized micro price theory, will reach equilibrium only when prices have been reduced to marginal costs. So Summers has general theory on his side when he asserts that "price will be bid down to marginal cost."

Because there is considerable leeway in different versions of theory about how marginal costs are defined, one must look to Summers's further statement to know how broadly or narrowly he defines the term. He adds "and the high initial fixed costs cannot be recouped"—meaning that these are not included in the marginal cost-based price. By so doing he adopts the narrow version of the definition that economists call "Short-Run Marginal Costs," abbreviated as SRMC.[8] Short-Run Marginal Costs covers only the *additional* or *incremental* costs—essentially the additional out-of-pocket costs—incurred to produce an additional unit (or group of units) of product.[9] As Alan Murray, a writer for the *Wall Street Journal* described, they are "the costs of producing and distributing, say, one more widget."[10] Prior investment costs, having already been incurred, do not increase with the addition of extra widgets, and so are not included in marginal costs.

An alternative distinction would define marginal costs as *variable* costs, changing with output, as contrasted with *fixed* costs, which remain constant over a broad range of outputs. Because fixed costs do not change as additional widgets are manufactured, the marginal costs of the added widgets do not include fixed costs. Such fixed costs are often referred to as "sunk" costs because the investments in facilities or knowl-

1. THE CHALLENGE TO ORTHODOXY • 9

edge, which they represent, have already been made, and therefore they are costs that exist regardless of future output.[11] Only variable costs are subject to the discretion of the producer, who is free to decide on the number of future widgets to be brought to the market. Under the fixed-variable terminology, Summers equates marginal costs to variable costs.

It is easy to grasp the importance of Summers's conclusion. Microsoft is a good illustration, although Summers shies away from mentioning any company by name. It seems to be generally conceded that Microsoft has invested huge sums on perfecting its various versions of Windows and its predecessors (although there may be much disagreement as to how "perfected" the end product is). Without the degree of monopoly power Microsoft has had or may have had—bypassing the "degree of power" controversy —Microsoft would have been faced with at least a partial and perhaps a total *non*recovery of its investment. Its per-unit price for Windows and its other software would have declined progressively to its negligible cost of cutting an extra copy of the program. This disastrous result would augur poorly for other would-be competitors. The hazards of launching a new product, or an improvement in an existing product, are ever present and unavoidable for venturesome entrepreneurs. If to this risk is added the likelihood that research and development and other startup investments will be stranded and unrecoverable per se because of enforced competition under the antitrust laws, the risk becomes overwhelming.

Permitting a temporary monopoly, with the promise that the government will not interfere by raising traditional antitrust objections, is Summers's solution. It would eliminate a powerful obstacle to continuity of the progress of innovation in the New Economy. That result would seem to be unarguable. What is arguable is whether the benefit achieved is, on balance, sufficient to override other benefits built into the antitrust laws that would be sacrificed.

That judgment might move in one direction or another depending upon whether a modification of the laws would extend to all industries, or apply only to information-type industries of the New Economy. The latter would be a compromise between conflicting principles—perhaps easier to sell politically, but certainly more difficult to define and administer. Summers does not mention any distinctions on coverage.

2. Reflections on the Summers Thesis

It is now appropriate to comment on several aspects of the Summers thesis that relate to marginal cost price theory (refer to "Notes on Theory" in chapter 3).

Prices Fall to Marginal Cost

Summers contends that without monopoly power, "price will be bid down to marginal cost and the high initial fixed costs cannot be recouped." This statement defines marginal cost as being the Short-Run Marginal Cost, or SRMC, of microeconomics. However, theory falls short of claiming that competitive prices will cover only SRMC. This low level is recognized in theory, but will occur *only* at equilibrium under the hypothetical condition of perfect competition. It is agreed, however, that the pressures of competition will *tend* to drive price downward, perhaps as low as marginal costs per the SRMC formula.[1] But the rapidity of the price reductions, and their lower limit, are unknown.

Further, there is little empirical evidence that prices in the competitive economy actually fall to mere out-of-pocket costs.

Robert M. Solow is one prominent economist who disagrees with the hypothesis that real-world prices necessarily will sink to marginal costs. He assumes a depressed economic condition—recession when prices would be expected to be at a low ebb—and asks this question:

> In any recession, it is all too obvious that most business firms would be happy to produce and sell more than they are currently able to sell at the current price. *Evidently, then, price exceeds marginal cost.* Why do firms not quote lower prices to increase sales? [emphasis added][2]

The answer might be inelastic demand, response of rivals to the price cut, annoyance of customers at later price increases, or any other reason for "price stickiness." Solow's point is clear, however: competitive prices may not sink to marginal costs. Actual competition does not conform to the "perfect competition" model.

Also, the rigid definition of marginal costs implied by Summers is not carved in stone. The most ardent advocate of marginal cost pricing, Alfred E. Kahn, does not insist on the total exclusion of fixed cost recovery even for the purpose of regulated prices aimed at the goal of "marginal cost pricing to attain economic efficiency." A "second best" alternative, Long-Run Marginal Costs or LRMC, provides much more leeway as to the costs to be considered in the marginal cost definition.

The Proposition Restated

These cautions suggest that there may be some oversimplification by Summers. But his fundamental proposition, which is paraphrased below, seems to be solid.

> Absent some degree of monopoly power, competition will *tend* to drive prices down to marginal cost, and in so doing *threaten* the recovery of sunk costs.[3] In the New Economy, this is a threat to the recovery of research and development outlays which are a key to continuing progress. Any such threat is a disincentive to new investment.

The foregoing paraphrase tempers the sweeping thrust of the Summers statement as he presented it, substituting a *tendency* toward marginal costs under competition, and a *threat* to recovery of sunk costs, for an asserted certainty of these results.

Resources Are Limited

Micro price theory begins with the central building-block proposition that society's resources are limited. From that proposition, it is concluded that the most efficient use of these limited resources should be the goal of price policy. In their joint paper, DeLong and Summers point out that this concept of limited resources does not necessarily apply in the New Economy. They comment:

> It is a principal characteristic of the new economy that my consumption of a good does not necessarily detract from your consumption of it. If I am wearing my shoe, you cannot be wearing my shoe. But if I am informed, if I have access to software, you can also have access to that software. . . . A world in which the information-technology sector is salient is one in which more of the goods that are produced will have the character of pharmaceuticals, or books, or records, in that they involve very large fixed costs and much smaller marginal costs. It is one in which positive network effects will be much more pervasive. . . .

> * * *

> The greater salience of these characteristics has crucial implications for business and for the functioning of the economy as a whole. The "new economy" will have more examples of very high fixed costs and very low marginal costs. Such a pattern can produce positive feedback.

This general proposition from theory is easy to accept when the resources are conceived of as being physical—natural resources such as iron or petroleum—with these resources being brought to the stage of consumer products by manufacturing or refining plant capacity, which themselves had required further use of our resource supplies.

This goal of efficient use also is easy to accept as applied generally to labor, particularly in a situation of national labor shortages (where unemployment is low over most of the workforce). It is less easy to grasp but equally valid in the opposite condition of a labor surplus (where unemployment is high), because this condition suggests the possibility of substituting additional labor in place of capital investment in labor-saving machinery or like measures. Over the years, the nation has experienced both conditions. There have been concerns that the economy has too few doctors or too many, too few engineers or too many, too few science teachers or too many, and so on for most of the professions; even a shortage or surplus of lawyers may have been experienced (although there may be few who argue for a shortage in this group). Untrained workers similarly may be in short or oversupply, notably in agriculture or lower paying jobs.

Today, concern seems to focus on a shortage of skilled computer talent, and the similar specialized talents, which comprise the broader worker pool for research and development (R&D).

This present shortage poses the question as to whether R&D, the product of the mind, may be a different kind of resource, not measurable by a numbers count to determine under- or over-supply. Certainly there is a shortage of Picasso paintings, judging by the market prices his works now command. Could a shortage of the products of this artistic genius have been avoided by pursuing a policy of encouragement of artists?

In today's terms, the dilemma may be comparable. If innovation is the goal, the genuinely creative innovator may be as rare among cyberspace talent as Picasso was among artists. The originality of concept, the genius that led to a Windows or a Linux operating system is not commonplace, and might not be appreciably expanded merely by increasing the number of available technicians.

Nonetheless, it is valid to hold as a goal the encouragement of the supply of technical talent for R&D. This might point to higher wages and fringe benefits for the R&D labor pool, which would increase R&D expenditures.[4] Higher outlays would cause recovery of R&D investment costs to be even more essential for a new firm's viability, and cause the threat of failure to recover to be more hazardous.[5] The joint Delong-Summers paper adds this comment: "In the new economy, it is clear that human capital is a strong complement to physical capital and intellectual capital."

On a broader basis, R&D has been an ingredient in the design and construction of the nation's enormous physical plant, and in the development of consumer products as well. That is not new for the New Economy. The New Economy, however, particularly if viewed as the Information Age, puts much greater reliance on R&D than in the past. This type of R&D does not deprive the world of its scarce physical assets in the sense of depleting a scarce supply. A ton of iron and a barrel of crude oil can be used only once.[6] In contrast, an innovative thought from a single mind can be repeatedly succeeded many times later by innovative thoughts from that same mind. The potential output of the mind is not exhausted, nor diminished in its value, by reason of its output.

The product of R&D in the New Economy is perishable, transitory. Today's results are likely to be outmoded by tomorrow's. This is not the case (at least to anywhere near the same degree) for the physical plant that supports our industrialized society. Electric power plants, buildings, and roads have a useful life expectancy of many years, not months or days.

To the extent that there is a meaningful difference between the New Economy and the old in this respect, the foregoing consideration supports the Summers thesis that it is counterproductive to continue an economic environment that allows prices to sink (or tend to sink) to SRMC, with doubtful recovery of R&D costs.

To explain the above conclusion, the theory is examined in different terms. Short-run marginal cost is a price goal directed toward the allocation of resources so as to conserve them for their most productive use. Using a resource for one purpose preempts its use for a different purpose. But use of the mind, particularly in innovative research, is not limited. R&D may begin with one objective, and discover others that are quite different. The goal should be to encourage R&D, not ration it. The New Economy should foster, not discourage, R&D cost recovery. At least for the innovative firm, price should not be bid down to SRMC.

Too Much Emphasis?

Entering with gusto into a new century, it is prudent to be cautious in emphasizing the new to the disregard of the old. The Summers proposition highlights the importance of fixed cost recovery as being essential for the New Economy. It is not a disagreement with Summers to note that such recovery is just as essential for established businesses. The change for the New Economy is a matter of degree.

In fact, recovery (or nonrecovery) of fixed costs in price is a concern of every business, old or new, large or small. Profitability depends upon the adequacy of price to cover costs.

The "change in degree" perception seems to boil down to the thought that R&D efforts will loom larger and be more expensive in the future than they have been in the past, while at the same time being more uncertain in terms of results and more transitory in terms of the benefits they bring to the originator. This combination of high risk and short duration of advantages gained moves much of the anticipated R&D into a speculative investment category. Hence, the argument goes, permitting a temporary monopoly is a desirable change in the antitrust laws because it would eliminate a *legal* threat to fixed cost recovery while not interfering with price competition from competitors. In this sense, it would be a double-pronged change. It would remove a legal threat to an existing enterprise that has already garnered some market power, but at the same time it would improve the climate for other enterprises seeking to gain the same market power for themselves.

Attention has been given in this volume and in the media to Microsoft and to prescription drugs as illustrations of the importance of R&D in major economic sectors. But fixed costs are not unique to R&D, nor to the software and pharmaceutical industries. They are pervasive, ubiquitous. Investments giving rise to fixed costs are required for every business, from Harry Truman's famed haberdashery to the massive capital-intensive industries. For former president Truman's shop they would be small; for a steel mill or an electric generating plant, they would be huge. In any case, except where a government subsidy is involved, their fixed costs must be recovered in price.

Even for Microsoft, its fixed costs do not arise exclusively from its R&D for Windows and its other products. Consider its extensive headquarters campus at Redmond, Washington. The structures there are physical plants of steel, concrete, and other materials too numerous to mention. The fixed costs of this physical plant also must be recovered in Microsoft's price. And further, included in the physical plant costs are the R&D investments made for its specific design, as well as hidden R&D costs previously made for the improvement of its input materials.

For the pharmaceutical industry also, the association of high fixed costs vis-à-vis R&D may be subject to exaggeration.

First, it is noted that new drugs may achieve the equivalent of a temporary monopoly by means of patents within existing law. These are intended to permit recovery of the sunk costs of research and development, and also, of course, to be an incentive for new products.[7] Regardless of these protections, drug companies, as others, always operate under the shadow of the threat of the antitrust statutes.

Second, it seems that current concerns of the drug industry are centered on the prevention of governmental control of drug prices, not on a relaxation of the antitrust laws. The July 6, 2000, *Wall Street Journal* reports: "Price controls, an idea once dismissed out of hand, are getting increasing political attention."[8]

Third, the same article in the *Wall Street Journal* foresees a change in direction by drug manufacturers. "The pharmaceutical industry is gradually shifting the core of its business from the unpredictable and increasingly expensive task of creating drugs and toward the steadier business of marketing them . . . more and more of the industry's research is being conducted in biotech labs." If this shift is occurring, a temporary monopoly exemption from antitrust might be of possible help to the small biotech firms, but might have little effect on easing the problem of high-cost prescription drugs sold by the majors.

Fourth, the R&D share of the drug industry's total costs seems to be greatly overstated in the public mind. Harris finds for the *Wall Street Journal*: "overall, the industry's marketing and administrative expenses are generally more than twice those of research and development."

In fact, it may be the case over the entire spectrum of competitive industries that the recent growth of marketing programs has outstripped the growth of R&D. Certainly, the influencing of consumer choice is the overwhelming message in current media advertising for drugs, software, and the like. But the strength of this message must rest ultimately upon the results of R&D.

This discussion of "Too Much Emphasis?" on R&D closes with the conclusion that permitting a temporary monopoly is a broad issue with many ramifications, not a simplistic question with easy answers.

Incentive

The thesis supporting a temporary monopoly supposes that a strong incentive for innovation would result from the lure offered to the innovator of the potential to charge prices inflated by market power without the threat of antitrust interference. This supposition necessarily assumes that a market for the product exists and that this market is strong enough to support prices at a market-power level. These are major assumptions. They postpone the prospect for profitability until after the product has been developed, produced, and offered for sale.

A strong argument can be made that this thesis is invalid, or of lesser importance to innovation than it is purported to be, at least in the case of the "dot.coms." There is much evidence to suggest the contrary for these emerging firms. It appears that the new innovators of Silicon Valley, and the venture capitalists who support them, look to short-term appreciation in stock market value as their incentive, not to more remote post–start-up prices and consequent operational profits.

Characteristically, the dot.coms have garnered sizable investor capital and have spent much of it, yet have neither a salable product nor an

existing market. Their chance is slim at best of ever reaching a position having market power and the ability of pricing to take advantage of it.
In mid-2000, *Business Week* looked back:[9]

> . . . only a matter of months ago . . . investors were beating down their doors to throw billions of dollars at every high-tech prodigy they could bring public . . .
>
> Every venture capitalist . . . eager to have the next America Online, Inc. or Amazon.com . . . tossed huge amounts of money at redundant companies in an attempt to outspend and underprice rivals.

At first glance, motivation dominated by the hope of stock value appreciation would seem to nullify any advantages to the New Economy of permitting a temporary monopoly for innovations in cyberspace and elsewhere. A more serious analysis suggests the reverse.

It is true that speculation has moved up the stock prices of numerous new ventures to unbelievable heights (noting that frantic hindsight has reduced them again to fractions of their former values). However, it is hard to accept speculation to this degree as representing a rational long-term market condition for the New Economy. The rational market supports enterprises that reasonably promise a profitable future. This promise can be fulfilled only with the expectation that prices will be adequate to recover both the sunk fixed costs of the past and the ongoing operating costs of the future. Full cost recovery might be possible only with some monopoly power. If the antimonopoly provisions of the antitrust laws are enforced rigidly, the requisite monopoly power might be considered a violation—a potent threat to full cost recovery.

As *Business Week* concludes in the article quoted above, "indiscriminate investing" is likely to be replaced by deciding which companies are "worth investing in for the long haul." The prospect of realizing full cost recovery is clearly a positive consideration in investor decisions; any legal bar is a negative threat. Long-term success of an emerging company's stock depends upon its prospects for viability when it becomes a going concern, and viability hinges on adequate prices, including profit, for its product.

Allocations

Summers's thesis seems to be a clear-cut recitation of fact: without temporary monopoly power, price will be bid down to marginal cost, and high initial fixed costs cannot be recouped. But this begs two un-avoidable questions for the multiproduct firm: (1) which product? and (2) which costs?

For Microsoft, the product might be its operating system, Windows, its word processing program, Word, or its tie to the world of cyberspace, Internet Explorer, to name a sampling. Or is "the" product some combination of closely intertwined products?

Micro theory demands the identification of the product (or products) being considered because marginal costs cannot be determined except for a specific unit of output or a specific service. "Which product?" must be answered.

The question of "which costs" is partially decided when a decision is made as to whether to follow SRMC or LRMC guidelines. But this is only a beginning.

Direct costs by definition are assignable without quibble to a specific product. For the single-product firm, all costs are direct. The only chore is to distinguish between variable and fixed costs.

The multiproduct firm presents costing problems that increase exponentially. Direct costs remain simple to assign, of course. Indirect (common) costs, incurred jointly for all products, require allocation among these products by some judgmental formula so as to pinpoint a cost for each.

Not entirely with tongue in cheek, Summers's generalized statement is expanded to make it more specific. A factory having an output of several products produced in common is assumed. The allocations of the common costs are illustrative.

> *Without temporary monopoly power* possessed by producer *xyz* for its product ABC, its *price* for that product *will be bid down to marginal cost* (which consists of 100 percent of its direct costs for the product, 34 percent of its common operations costs, 42.5 percent of its common maintenance costs, 5 percent of its overhead costs, and [to account for increased depreciation] 1.25 percent of its fixed non-R&D capital costs) *and the high initial fixed costs* (consisting of 100 percent of its R&D and other investment costs, plus the residual portions of the common costs listed above, viz., 66 percent of common operations, 57.5 percent of common maintenance, 95 percent of overhead, and 98.75 percent of fixed non-R&D capital costs) *cannot be recouped except* as higher than marginal cost prices can be charged to its other products. (emphasis in original)

The substance of the above is that for the multiproduct firm *all* variable costs for an individual product (or function) other than those that are directly assignable, must be calculated by arbitrary (judgmental) allocation. (If investment [capital] costs were to be included in whole or part, these also would have to be allocated among the common products.)

The above illustration is in no way intended to question the essential logic of the Summers thesis, which (modified as suggested earlier) is sound. The purpose of the illustration is simply to point out the difficulties.

Nature of the Monopoly

The Summers solution itself is not as simple as implied by the recommendation, "grant a temporary monopoly." An example will illustrate this, assuming a multiproduct firm. A temporary monopoly for product A of a multiproduct firm would have to distinguish between (1) the costs of product A, which would be exempted from scrutiny under the antitrust statutes, and (2) the costs, and the prices associated therewith, of products B, C, D . . . N, which would not be exempt. Without this distinction, some costs properly associated with products B, C, D . . . N might be transferred to product A, with the result that product A would cross-subsidize the other products, in effect extending the same temporary monopoly exemption to these other products. It is hard to believe that such cross-subsidy would not be challenged in an antitrust context.

Continuing this same illustration, suppose a temporary monopoly were to be given to an entire firm, covering all of its products or services, both those presently offered and any new innovations of the future. In the extreme, this would effectively sanction any market power influencing the price of each and every one of its products, removing all of its prices from possible question by competitors. Or, if challenge was permitted, the same cost morass would need to be resolved.

Finally, if a temporary monopoly were to be given to an entire industry as distinct from a specific firm or firms—however unlikely that might be—it does not necessarily follow that the cost morass would be avoided. A definition of the protected industry would be required, as would a delineation of its protected prices, unless the antitrust laws were to be extinguished in their entirety. These definitions would by necessity rest upon a cost analysis foundation. Otherwise an exempted manufacturer (say, of software) could intermingle with impunity its costs of software, and its software prices, with its costs, and its prices, for an entirely different function (say, of computer manufacturing and distribution). Clearly, such a cost analysis foundation would be challengeable at the outset of its introduction before the Congress and later before the courts.

It is concluded that costing problems are unavoidable. Fortunately, marginalism may provide a blueprint for future guidance.

Views in Common, Yet Apart

It is interesting to observe that the Summers thesis and normative economic theory converge on important basics, but reach opposite conclusions.

Price Signals

Both Summers and normative economics recognize the importance of price signals as economic policy indicators, but they view the signals differently. Summers contends that a price that is unprotected by a temporary monopoly privilege signals the possibility (and eventually the certainty) that the price will fall to bare marginal cost, and therefore foreclose for the enterprise a full recovery of its fixed costs. The signal conveys bad news, discouraging future investment, and, hence, damaging the New Economy.

The traditional economic position, on the other hand, contends that a marginal cost price sends good news to the economy, old or new without differentiation, because it makes it possible for consumers to adjust their buying habits so as to result in an efficient allocation of resources (economic efficiency).

Capital-Intensive Industries

These two versions of economics also have a similar focus. Both seem concerned with industries that are capital intensive, but look in different directions.

Looking toward the New Economy, Summers is concerned with enterprises whose capital needs are heavy to support intensive investment in research and development (computer software, prescription drugs, etc.). This type of investment is needed, he says, for rapid innovation that will be the wellspring of the New Economy.

Alfred E. Kahn, who introduced marginal cost into the forefront of regulated pricing for utilities, holds the opposite view. Kahn, whose interest lies in the most effective allocation of society's limited resources overall, also concentrates on capital-intensive industries (the utilities), but where the high level of investment arises from the construction of plant capacity.

From these different perspectives, these two highly qualified economists reach completely opposing opinions regarding the role of marginal cost pricing.[10]

Summers sees a marginal cost-based price as a deterrent to growth in the economy; Kahn, as an essential for the health of the economy. They agree that a continuing flow of new investment is required, and would apparently agree that some of these new dollars will finance research and development while others will finance provision of plant capacity (although they could be expected to disagree about the relative proportions of these alternative dispositions in the mix). The cause célèbre of their divergence seems to be *incentive*: lacking in a marginal cost-based price, according to Summers; adequate, per Kahn.[11]

Trial Balloon?

The intent of Summers in making his "temporary monopoly" remarks is still unclear as of this writing. It is uncertain whether he meant to launch a movement toward a change in the antitrust laws (or at least a less rigid interpretation of these laws) for serious debate as a major public policy issue, or whether he meant merely to let loose a trial balloon to test uncertain waters.

Regardless of his intent, a challenge to orthodoxy of this magnitude cannot be dismissed. The Justice Department cannot simply shove under the rug comments of a high government official (even though he may no longer be in office) that are adverse to Justice's position in many pending matters. Neither can the economics profession lightly dismiss the implications on micro theory posited by a knowledgeable member of its own ranks.

Others are implicated also: the securities market in general and venture capitalists in particular; the software industry and its innovators; the pharmaceutical industry and its researchers, as well as their clientele, users of prescription drugs; dot.coms in whatever field. The list goes on and on: it is a listing of all emerging participants in the New Economy.

But the Old Economy is not exempt. Research and development is necessary for *most* industries, old as well as new, and *all* industries face the problem of recovering their fixed (sunk) costs in their prices. This universality of interest spreads the implications of the Summers thesis over the entirety of the U.S. economy, and, indirectly, throughout the industrialized world.

The joint paper adds a further important dimension, implicit but not highlighted in Summers's 2000 statements. This points to the broader role of intellectual property, property rights, and innovation as policy concerns. The paper includes the following analysis:

> The most critical issues are those that revolve around intellectual property. It is a fact that we today simply do not know yet how to make the intellectual property system work for the new economy. . . .
>
> Today it appears that intellectual property is rapidly becoming a much more important source of value. One response would be to reinforce the rights of "owners." The underlying idea is that markets work because everything is someone's property. Property rights give producers the right incentives to make, and users the right incentives to calculate, the social cost of what they use. It is clear that without strong forms of protection of property rights, a great many useful products would never be developed at all. This principle applies as strongly to intellectual as to other forms of property.
>
> But with information goods the social marginal cost of distribution is close to zero. One of the most fundamental principles of economics is that prices should be equal to social marginal cost. In this case, strong intellectual property rights have the potential to decrease economic efficiency by driving prices away from marginal social cost.
>
> Thus different economic principles cut in different directions. If information goods are to be distributed at their marginal cost of production—zero—they cannot be created and produced by entrepreneurial firms that use revenues obtained from sales to consumers to cover their costs. If information goods are to be created and produced by businesses that face the right incentives to explore new paths, they must be able to anticipate selling their products at a profit to someone. . . . Mainstream academic economics has long underestimated the importance of Hayekian insights into market competition as a discovery mechanism, of the entrepreneurial advantages of private enterprise, and of the administrative defects of overly-rigid systems of top-down control that come with centralized funding (see Scott 1998).
>
> We know that markets and the spur of competition are the best producers of applied knowledge. But we do not know how to use markets and competition for this purpose as far as information goods are concerned, and still satisfy the economic principle that final consumers should pay no more than marginal cost.

At the same time, we also know that the Lockeian belief that property rights are good, that intellectual property is a form of property like any other, and thus that stronger intellectual property rights are good, is simply wrong. In the "Smithian" economy, property rights are good because they (a) force buyers to pay prices for goods, and thus to approximately internalize in their own decision making the effect of their actions in reducing the ability of others to use scarce, rival goods, and (b) allow for the decentralization of economic decisions and thus for entrepreneurship. In the "new economy," with nonrival goods, property rights that force buyers to pay prices above very low marginal cost do not contribute to but detract from economic efficiency, and lead not to decentralization but to a greater degree of centralization in economic decision making in the hands of the owner of the intellectual property rights.

Complicating the issues still further, the most important innovations that we see today are built on progress in basic science, everything from group theory to quantum theory. If one asked what research had made the most important contribution to the navigation of ships since the 1600s, a good case could be made that it was pure mathematics. . . . We know from long experience that basic science is best diffused broadly, so production must be supported from the outside. That is why a crucial component of public policy at this time must be strong support for basic research.

Moreover, basic research must be widely disseminated because basic research and applied research are cumulative enterprises. There is a good chance that heavy restrictions on the dissemination of intellectual property will do less to create incentives for research and development and more to destroy the web of scientific and technical communication that make research and development effective. . . .

New institutions and new kinds of institutions—perhaps some that have been tried before . . . may well be necessary to achieve the fourfold objectives of (a) price equal to marginal cost, (b) entrepreneurial energy, (c) accelerating the cumulative process of research, and (d) providing appropriate financial incentives for research and development. . . .

These are the ramifications, the ripple effects, of a seemingly simple statement.

Many will engage in support; many will rise in opposition. Who these will be is unknown. It seems clear only that few will be able to abstain.

So, let the debate begin.

3. Marginal Costs and Marginalism
Background and Application

Overview

Marginal Cost in the New Economy proposes that marginal cost techniques be adopted as a standard for policy evaluation. It explores how marginal cost principles and methodology could be a useful tool for the economic analysis of current and emerging public policy issues such as school vouchers and the encouragement of innovation. It also examines how the marginalist approach could improve the analysis of ever-present recurring issues, including those related to mergers, patent extensions, and antitrust.

The prospective major role of marginalist practices would be to provide a uniform theoretically sound yardstick for economic evaluations of policy issues, whether new or recurring. This yardstick would measure costs and prices when these are significant inputs into the pros and cons of a proposed policy or a debatable regulatory decision. *It is designed to mesh traditional theory with modern requirements, such as those mentioned by Summers.*

The value of a uniform yardstick for cost and price evaluation hardly needs emphasis. Confusion reigns absent a consistent standard, as was recently impressed upon the nation by the controversy over Florida's ballot counting in the 2000 presidential election. Is a dimple or a pregnant chad a vote? In economic parallel, what is cost? In sum, it is suggested that marginalist procedures (marginalism) be adopted to supersede hit-and-miss approaches.

As background, this chapter reviews current dogma on marginal costs, and outlines principles that should govern their application as a yardstick.

Marginalism: An Approach and a Method

Strictly defined, *marginal cost* is the extra (or incremental) cost of producing an extra unit of output (the marginal unit). This definition is also applicable in its opposite, the cost saved by producing one less unit, usually called the avoided cost. Bringing together these elements, marginal cost is the cost incurred, or the cost saved, in the production of the marginal unit of output.

The typical example is a manufacturing firm. Assume a factory is currently producing one million units a year, but is considering increasing production by 100,000 units (or decreasing production by 100,000 units). In either case, the marginal change in production would be 100,000 units. The marginal cost would be the extra cost incurred (or avoided) by reason of this change in output.

This strict definition is limiting, in that it implies that marginal cost is applicable only to a production process (such as manufacturing and mining).

Marginal cost is viewed herein in a broader light, for which the term *marginalism* (or *marginal analysis*) is adopted. As generally defined in the literature, the term represents a comparison of marginal benefits (extra benefits) and marginal costs (added costs), resulting from a departure from a given position (which may be a change from the status quo, a change in governmental or corporate policy, or a weighting of alternative policies). This is the concept underlying the familiar cost-benefit ratio. It is an extension of marginal cost in the strict sense in that it takes into account the effects of *all* major changes, including benefits, not just changes in costs incurred or avoided due to output variations.

Two requirements are added to the above definition. These additional requirements are not necessarily included in the typical cost-benefit ratio.[1] In fact, they are often ignored. They are, first, that the elements entering into the analysis should look *to the future*, not back, and second, that these elements be measured on their impact *at the margin*, rather than in total.[2]

With these requirements added, marginalism carries forward the fundamental marginal cost precept that the most significant results of a change (from one pattern of operations, services, or policies to another) are those that occur *at the margin*, these being the effects that directly flow from the change, for which the change is causally responsible. The change itself may be a shift in policy, consideration of the relative impacts of different policies, product improvement, an increase or decrease in output, a new service or a new product, and so forth. Whatever the change, the analyst concentrates on the identification and measurement of its marginal effects.

Where products are considered, the relevant future market is the market for the incremental output, with consideration of the impacts, if any, on related markets. The relevant costs are the costs incurred (or avoided) by the change. Relevant benefits are the revenues added (or lost). Revenues and costs may be computed on a per-unit-of-product or a total basis. The latter is preferred, and conforms to the academic definition of marginal impact as the rise or fall in total costs, and, if appropriate, in total revenues. Whichever is used (and they should net to the same amounts), the marginalist compares the increase (or decrease) in revenues resulting from the change with the associated increase (or decrease) in costs.

Where policies, as distinct from products, are involved, the analysis is more complex. The starting point will be a base reflecting future costs and future benefits as they would be with the present policy kept in place. From this point, each marginal effect must be identified and quantified as a future change in cost or benefit. Externalities should be included to the extent practicable.

Marginalism is both an approach and a method. It means, in essence, focusing upon the impact of an incremental change from a given base, whether that base be a production level, a services-offered level, or a policy. It also means looking forward in measuring the impacts, rather than back. Thus, the marginal benefits entering into a cost-benefit comparison are those expected to be gained or lost (regardless of historical benefits), while the costs incurred or saved are those actually anticipated (regardless of historical costs).

To clarify the difference between the limited and broader concepts of marginal costs, refer back for comparison to the prior illustration of the factory's change in output. Assume the firm to be a service provider, issuing medical insurance. It is considering extending its present coverage by adding prescription drugs, dental care, or any other new service (or by dropping a service previously offered). The marginal change in services offered would be the addition (or deletion) of the specific service in question. Determining the marginal costs incurred or avoided by the change would be enough to satisfy the strict definition. But the concept of marginalism goes further.

Adding or dropping a service influences the attractiveness of the insurer's package of coverages. If made more attractive because of the service addition, the insurer's overall costs and revenues will both be higher, hopefully showing a *net* improvement. If made less attractive because of the service deletion, overall costs and revenues will be less, possibly showing a *net* loss. Each of these would be the direct effect of the change in the marginal service offering. Changes up or down in marginal costs alone constitute only a part of the marginal effects. Altered revenues and other cost revisions are also relevant to the cause-and-effect scenario of marginalism.

Value Judgments Excepted

The approach as a generality seems to fit most conditions. But application of the methodology in any refined sense may be illusive if not impossible under other conditions. Application is particularly difficult when shifts in broad policy, whether governmental or corporate, are under consideration.

A governmental policy change is perhaps the most complex. The change may set in motion widespread ripple effects that seem to go on and on without end. Others have impacts that are almost impossible to measure on a tangible dollars-and-cents basis. Some combine both characteristics.

In these circumstances, how extensive, or how limited, are the effects to be considered? Of course, there is no single answer. The general rule, mentioned earlier, is that an effect should be included if, and only if, the policy change in question is *causally responsible* for the change in costs or benefits.

An example of a complex policy change is President Clinton's executive order, issued shortly before he left office, which restricted future use of U.S. forest lands. The order banned cutting, road construction, and commercial development in certain areas, limited "stewardship logging," and banned commercial logging in roadless sections of national forests.

Broadly observed, this executive order presumably reflects the president's decision that the long-term benefits to the public of keeping federal lands in pristine condition (the main marginal benefit, possibly increased by lower maintenance costs, savings from eliminating new road construction, etc.) offset any disadvantages to the public (marginal costs) such as limited public access and increased fire hazards due to lack of roads, loss of jobs, loss of revenues from timber sales, and so forth.

Because the main factors on either side of the decision—benefits or detriments to the public—are intangible and thus elude precise analysis, the president's decision is a *value judgment,* which economics cannot say is right or wrong. (This is not to overlook the probability that a thousand pages of "environmental impact statement" will be written in support, and an equal number of pages in opposition, as this executive order is tested in the courts or in Congress.)

Public and Corporate Policy

Although the methodology is equally appropriate for both corporate policy evaluations and policies in the public sector, the latter is emphasized for two reasons.

First, uniformity and consistency in public policy formulation is of prime importance because of the intertwining of governmental activities with one another. There is overlap within the same jurisdictional area (such as diverse federal activities, supervised by different departments in a given region) where policies should mesh, not conflict, with each other. There is the same overlap between jurisdictions, such as between federal and state, and state and local. While no methodology can by itself eliminate inconsistencies, a uniform approach coupled with a uniform method can be a first step toward minimizing contradictory policies.

Second, there is a major difference in objectives between public and corporate goals. The broad goal of policies directing the government should be the public interest at large. Corporate policy is narrower, focusing primarily on the welfare of the firm and its stockholders. Except as guided by the invisible hand, the two goals do not mix. One recalls the famous statement of a high business executive: "What's good for General Motors is good for the country." Perhaps. In any event, public policies on the whole are seen as a macro issue, while corporate policies, regardless of the size and influence of the corporation, are micro.

If these differences are valid, why is it recommended that the approach and the method be followed in both sectors? Here, again, there are two reasons.

First, private policies must coexist with public policies. Private interests should be heard, for example, when governmental regulations are being framed and enforced. The best way to reach an accommodation between opposing points of view is for the opposing parties to start from common ground. To hold its own, the private party should be expert in the government's methods. This would seem to be particularly crucial in antitrust disputes. Ignorance is not bliss!

Second, the approach and methodology yield "best option" results when alternative policies are being weighed. This applies to corporate as well as to public-sector determinations. To elaborate on the preceding point, a proposed corporate action, such as a merger, might have a better chance of approval if supported by the uniform methodology, showing it to be attractive both to the corporate and the public welfare, each showing emerging from the same concept of "best option."

Earlier, the Summers proposal has been highlighted. This would grant a temporary monopoly to innovative firms for the purpose of shielding these firms from prices that might be bid down to marginal costs, which price level would foreclose recovery of fixed costs, including recovery of already-incurred expenditures for research and development. Nonrecovery of sunk costs would obviously be detrimental to the availability of new capital, whether such capital was governmental or private.

Tampering with the antitrust laws, whether relaxing or tightening, is clearly a major public policy decision. A change such as suggested by Summers must necessarily be the subject of extensive debate. Marginalism as a principle should shape the argument. On the cost side will be the excess of the higher monopoly price over the lower competitive price for each prescription drug (or other product) during the patent period. On the benefit side will be the value of the improvement in public health expected to result from an accelerated flow of new or improved drugs. Many values on each side might be either speculative or intangible, so the Summers issue may have to be resolved as a value judgment. Even for a value judgment, the marginalist approach has the additional merit of imposing discipline on both sides. Neither can stray from including as costs or benefits *only* those causally related to the change. A haphazard listing of all conceivable costs or benefits, marshaled argumentatively on either side to gain an extra point, would be ruled out.

Prices and Costs

A fundamental fact of economic analysis underlies all of the foregoing: *It is impossible to deal intelligently at the policy level with price-linked issues without knowledge of costs. Cost and price are inseparable.*

A price standing alone tells nothing. It may be too high, too low, or just about right. Two different prices standing together also tell nothing. Is either too high or too low? Are both too high or too low? Or is one or the other just about right? A price can be evaluated for reasonableness only in terms of the costs that it is designed to cover: without a knowledge of these costs, a price is impossible to interpret.

Let us take the Summers issue of a temporary monopoly for a product. Assume price X for a product under temporary monopoly protection. Further assume a lower price Y without such protection. Is the difference in price, X minus Y, too much to pay for the advantages to the public gained in granting the monopoly to X? This cannot be answered except by a wild guess, for we do not know what the X and Y prices will be. But it is possible to calculate what they might be, at least at the extremes.

For purposes of this calculation, we can assume that the X price might include all variable costs plus investment and infrastructure costs (including R&D) plus other constant costs, such as overheads, including a "normal" or higher profit. This would be a maximum figure.

For the Y price, we can assume only the coverage of all variable costs. This would be a minimum figure.

On the basis of this maximum for the high price and this minimum for the low, it is possible to estimate the highest reasonable overage of X over Y. There is now a basis for debate, although all figures are (unfortunately) subject to contest.

The lower price, Y, benefits consumers in the short run, but exposes them to two different types of future risk. The first risk is that the concerned manufacturer will hesitate to build new plant or to undertake new research and development because its costs for that effort will not be covered in its price for its newly discovered products. The second risk is industrywide. The concerned industry may fail to attract new investment necessary for continued growth, eventually becoming dormant.

The higher price, X, benefits consumers in the longer run because it promises continued infusions of capital to both the concerned manufacturer and the concerned industry, and holds the promise of bringing to the public new and innovative products.

Is the difference in price, X minus Y, in the public interest? Economists might advance their opinions (and undoubtedly would). But the final answer will come from the policy makers in government. They alone have the authority. The role of economists is to provide solid data for policy makers, not to make final decisions.

The above observations on the price-cost link are presented as a helpful illustration. But it is repeated once again, that the need for solid data can best be met by following a uniform method for cost analysis, which would eliminate, or at least lessen, the wide disparities in cost results occurring from different approaches to the calculation of costs.

Notes on Theory

Marginal costs occupy center stage in current microeconomic price theory. This theory, simplistically stated in many modern micro textbooks, declares that prices should be set at the level of marginal costs in order to attain economic efficiency.

The logic of the theory is simple. Marginal cost-based prices send accurate "price signals" to consumers. Having such accurate signals, consumers can evaluate a given product or service in proper perspective relative to alternative products or services. Thus, the buying decisions of consumers direct "the use of society's limited resources in such a way as to maximize consumer satisfaction." Such a maximum represents "economic efficiency."

The theory stems from the concept that productive resources are limited, and that pricing policy should be aimed at making the most effective use of these limited resources. In a competitive economy, consumers direct the use of resources by their buying choices. When they buy any given product, or buy more of that product, they are directing the economy to produce less of other products. The production of other products must be sacrificed in favor of the chosen product.

From this point, marginal cost theory takes a giant step. In essence, it states that if consumers are to choose rationally whether to buy more or less of any product, the price they pay should equate to the cost of supplying more or less of that product. This cost is the marginal cost of the product. *If consumers are charged this cost, optimum quantities will be purchased, maximizing consumer satisfaction.* If they are charged more, less than optimum quantities will be purchased: The sacrifice of other foregone products will have been overstated. If they are charged less, the production of the product will be greater than optimum: Sacrifice of the foregone products will have been understated. A price based on marginal costs is presumed to convey "price signals" that will lead to the efficient allocation of resources. This is the theory in brief, as drawn from the microeconomic model of pricing under perfect competition.[3]

This theory contends that prices under competition will sink to marginal cost, or have a tendency to do so. However, an important qualification is noted. The theory assumes conditions of "perfect competition," which are far removed from the conditions of "monopolistic (or imperfect) competition" which actually prevail. Consumer preferences for entrenched brand-name products, for example, may permit a supplier to charge prices above marginal cost for these products. Eventually, however, competitors will introduce and promote their own branded products, which again will bring into play active price competition, and again force (or tend to force) prices downward toward marginal cost.

The Future

A pervasive thread linking the several elements of the theory is the concept that pricing should look to the future, disregarding the past. It is held that only future costs should be reflected in price. These are the only costs over which the producer has control. He has no control over past costs, which are "sunk." These past costs, mainly fixed in nature, arise from invested capital that is already committed. Price, then, should be set by the producer *at any given time* in view of his future costs over which he has control. His sunk (fixed) costs are disregarded.

The logic of this assertion is dependent upon the companion proposition that the producer also has no control over the prices that will be offered by competitors, who similarly will look to their future costs in setting their prices and similarly will disregard their sunk costs.

Incentive

Clearly, the thought that investment costs will not be recovered in prices (absent some sanction of "monopoly power" in pricing), falls short of providing incentive for new investment. For this reason the recovery, or nonrecovery, of sunk costs is a controversial element of the theory among economists.

Time Frames

Marginal cost prices, as mentioned by Summers (chapter 1), exclude recovery of sunk costs ("high initial fixed costs cannot be recouped"). Marginal costs in this definition are reported in the literature as "Short-Run Marginal Costs" or SRMC. This short-run definition has been accepted ·by some regulatory commissions, including California, as their pricing goal.

An alternative definition, a "second best" approach, has been adopted by other regulatory commissions, "Long-Run Marginal Costs" or LRMC. As these titles indicate, the two versions differ in their time perspective, and hence in the costs to be included as marginal. With an apology for the present simplifications, SRMC includes only the out-of-pocket or variable costs incurred in changing output from one level to another. The time frame is the immediate present.

Long-run marginal cost looks forward further, for an indeterminate period. In its extreme version, it would cover all costs, capital as well as operating, that would be incurred in production of a forecasted output from a modern plant. Past fixed costs would be disregarded, but all future fixed costs would be included. This substitution might result in equivalent fixed costs, or be higher or lower, but the reality of capital costs would not be ignored. The difficulty with LRMC is that all costs are conjectural, each subject to question.

Between these two extremes is the "Intermediate-Run Marginal Cost" or IRMC. The time frame for IRMC is the near present as contrasted with the immediate present of SRMC.

Obviously, the short-run and the long-run versions are worlds apart.

Measurement

Previously, short-run marginal costs have been defined as being essentially out-of-pocket costs, variable in nature. This is useful as a rough definition. The more precise definition, which would have to be followed in any formal calculation, is that marginal cost is the change in total costs from one level of output to another, presumably (but not necessarily) an increase with a higher output, or a decrease with a reduced output. Measurement of the change in total costs is required for both SRMC and LRMC.

A total cost computation is always tricky. It includes noncash items, such as depreciation (a recapture of the investment), and a reasonable return on investment, that is, profit. These figures are always controversial.

A casual glance at SRMC might suggest that a total cost computation is unnecessary to determine the variable costs involved in the short run. This might be true if these short-run marginal costs were not subject to verification. However, verification undoubtedly would be required if the marginal cost figure was to be used for any legal purpose, such as in predatory pricing litigation. Here, the dispute might center on whether the accused producer was offering prices below its marginal cost to unfairly injure competitors (predatory pricing) or was simply setting its price with the legitimate goal of meeting competitors' prices.

Cost Allocations

Generalized designations of different kinds of costs and their measurement are deceptively simplistic. It should be easy and noncontroversial to identify particular costs as operating, capital, and so on. And it is easy, at least relatively so, for single-product firms, producing, say, bags of cement, each bag being the same as all other bags.

Unfortunately, however, single-product firms are rare in today's economy. Multiproduct firms dominate. Because products are individually priced, marginal costs for each separate product are required to implement the theory.

Some costs are *direct*. They arise in connection with a given product and no other. They can be assigned directly to that product: The cost of an ingredient purchased for a certain drug is a part of the marginal cost of that drug. This cost rises or falls with changes up or down in the volume of the drug produced. It is *variable* with production.

Direct variable costs are no problem. The problem arises because many (perhaps most) of the costs of a multiproduct firm are *common* to more than one product. These common costs must be apportioned, or allocated, among its products. Overheads are often cited as common costs: What proportion of the president's salary should be assigned to each product?

For a joint-product firm, this means that a marginal cost for Product A will consist of its direct costs plus an allocation of the common costs that are incurred for Products B, C, and D, as well as A.

The electric industry is a good example. Its plant consists of generating, transmission, and distribution facilities, which provide power to diverse types of customers (residential, commercial, and large and small industrial), in winter and in summer, during peak load periods as well as off peak. So what is the marginal cost of supplying (1) a residential customer, (2) in the summer, (3) at the time of the seasonal peak, with (a) generating, (b) transmission, and (c) distribution capacity, and (d) operation and maintenance of this capacity, all required to serve the customer? It is not necessary to belabor the point that the required marginal cost is the result of a series of allocations, each judgmental and each open to dissent. This is the dilemma posed by marginal costs for the multiproduct firm (or by any other type of costs, for that matter).

The Steps

Keeping in mind that there will be inevitable differences in each evaluation study, the procedural steps for a base-type study are outlined in generalized fashion below.

Step 1. Defining the Problem

It is desirable at the outset to clearly set forth the desired end result of the study. While this should be obvious, if it is overlooked, confusion is likely to occur in the course of the study, fogging its ultimate conclusions. For example, in the case of a specific software program, the specific program (or group of related programs) must be carefully identified. This may not be easy, but it will not be easier if postponed.

The case of an HMO's fees for care is a realistic example. Presumably the fee will cover specific multiple services, such as hospitalization, surgery, doctor visits for treatment and consultation, ambulance transportation, and so on. Prescription drugs may or may not be covered in the fee. Each of these multiple services has a separate cost (comprising the price paid by the HMO to its supplier) and the HMO's own overhead, each service having a separate frequency or volume of use. Patient coverage, both allowances and limitations, may vary from one patient classification to another. Whatever the range of services and patients to be studied may be, whether narrow or broad, these should be specified, together with a list of those to be ignored. Do the inclusions make sense in relation to the exclusions? In short, which services, which patients?

Step 2. Choosing the Time Frame

The appropriate time frame, SRMC, IRMC, or LRMC, will largely depend upon the purpose of the study. Generally speaking, IRMC gives greater flexibility than SRMC. It may be useful to analyze two time frames, both the short run and the intermediate run, as will be done in the school voucher study of chapter 5.

A full LRMC probably is the least useful for an analysis of public policy issues, for a long-run perspective becomes highly speculative and hard for the general public to accept.

A key time frame issue is the treatment of *investment costs*. For shorter-run time frames, SRMC or IRMC, investment costs are assumed to be fixed. That is, changes because of an increase or decrease in output are assumed to be made only *within the capabilities of the existing physical plant*. Appropriate changes in the operations of that plant can be made, such as adding or dropping a work shift, provided the existing plant itself is kept intact. For this reason, the base methodology does not take into account possible changes in the investment base.

An extended long-run view, LRMC, would envision plant changes, and corresponding changes in investment (capital) costs, as new state-of-the-art equipment might be substituted for less efficient equipment, or as the plant might be expanded or contracted. Economists are fond of saying, "in the long run, all costs are variable," indicating that over time the nature and extent of the capital required to conduct the enterprise will change.

Changes in investment costs introduce numerous difficult-to-evaluate questions into a marginal costs analysis (or any other type of analysis, for that matter). For this reason, further discussion of investment changes is postponed until later chapters.

Step 3. Defining the Unit of Measurement

The unit of measurement will vary to comport with the desired end result. In many cases the analyst has a choice. For a prescription drug, for example, the unit might be either (1) the cost of a single pill or a single injection, of uniform content, regardless of the frequency of the patient's use (making the medication cost to the patient different for each illness), or (2) the cost of the drug per month (or other appropriate period) for a specific illness (making the medication cost the same for all patients having the same illness).

Steps 1, 2, and 3 go hand in hand. They are not necessarily sequential.

Step 4. Obtaining the Basic Cost Data

This fourth step is likely to be the most difficult and frustrating. The concerned entity, whether it is a government agency or a private corporation, can be expected to be less than eager to release cost data, even if it has the data on hand (and it may not). Reluctance arises because of the suspicion that in some way the study may undermine the originator's own position. This reluctance is universal. Beyond that, corporations may regard their data as proprietary, not to be publicized, particularly to competitors or customers. Government data is not supposed to be secret, but the analyst will soon learn that it is not easy to pry loose.

Because of the difficulty in obtaining the basic cost data, it might be argued that this Step 4 should be listed as the first step. Perhaps this is simply the question, "which comes first, the chicken or the egg?" It is put in fourth place because requests for data should be framed in terms of the study's requirements, not the reverse. The analyst's initial request for a complete set of data may be the one and only chance of obtaining what is needed. Supplemental requests should be confined to fill in or refine the original. In other words, the analyst should do her or his homework before submitting a request.

The validity of the study rests upon the accuracy and completeness of the basic cost data that are its foundation. This goes without saying. The analyst must shoulder the responsibility for checking the data for inconsistencies. These are to be expected, especially so if it has been prepared by more than one source within the originating entity, or if data from different entities are to be combined.

The data request should ask for *costs by function,* which indicate the nature of the activities for which the costs were incurred. In marginalist terms, the cost breakdowns should be sufficiently precise to point to the activity (function) that has "causal responsibility" for the cost.

Unfortunately, conventional accounting often falls short of functionalization. The request may have to ask for (i.e., beg for) a special effort by the subject entity.

Step 5. Cost Classification

For multiproduct firms or multiservice government agencies, it is to be expected that activities related to more than one product or service will be conducted in the same facilities, and that the same employee may participate jointly in producing the output of more than one product or service. This likelihood requires that individual costs be classified as direct or common.

Direct costs are those that are associated with the production of only one product or service. They can be assigned directly and in their entirety to that product or service. *Indirect* or *common* costs are those that cannot be directly assigned to any single product or service by reason of the fact that the cost function contributes to the production of more than one, or is conducted in jointly used space or with jointly used equipment. The portion of these mixed or common costs that should be assigned to the product or service under consideration can be determined only by allocation.

Step 6. Cost Allocations

It is axiomatic that cost allocations are unavoidably and inevitably subjective, judgmental. Therein lies the problem. The analyst must select a reasonable, rational allocation method with the realization that affected parties may contest the choice, particularly if the choice leads to results that they would like to avoid. These parties are likely to suggest an alternative method that better suits their own purposes.

The only advice that can be given on this score is that the analyst caution himself or herself to be unbiased, with no preconceived cost result in mind. The objective should not be a high cost (leading to a high price) or a low cost (suggesting a low price). A preconceived end result should not enter into the analyst's choice of method.

A common error is to choose a simplistic method that is circular in its reasoning. Using relative revenues received from the several common products as a basis for allocation is an example. This is circular. Revenues reflect market prices, but prices themselves are the objective of the study.

A variety of allocation methods will occur to the analyst after observing the operations of the subject firm or agency. The golden rules for the selection are: (1) choose a method that is easily explained, and (2) choose the simplest method that is reasonably valid.

Step 7. Cost Selection

Because marginal methodology measures the change in cost that accompanies a change in output, only variable costs—those that vary with output—are relevant. But not all variable costs enter into every marginal cost analysis. For the multiproduct enterprise, only those variable costs that vary with the output of the subject product or service need be considered. Those that vary because of other factors are not pertinent.

For example, lighting and heating energy costs for a manufacturing facility will increase if the facility increases its operating hours, from one to two shifts, from a five-day-per-week schedule to a seven-day-per-week schedule, and so on. Energy costs of the factory are thus variable with its hours of operation. However, it is quite possible that the factory's operating hours will not change by reason of a change in the output of the subject product. Other products may necessitate continuity of the factory's operations at preexisting levels. In this instance, lighting and heating energy costs, while variable in nature, are irrelevant to the subject product and need not be considered. So the selection process consists of identifying the costs that vary with the subject product or service, eliminating other variable costs that do not.

Many costs are semivariable and semifixed, having characteristics of both. As with allocations, how to classify such costs is a subjective, judgmental matter. The ultimate classification may depend upon the time frame of the study. As illustrated in the school voucher analysis, many costs may be considered to be "sticky" in the short run but variable in the intermediate run. Other costs may be fixed in either of the two shorter-run scenarios, but variable over a longer-term period.

Regardless of the time frame, the rule is: Select costs for all activities that are causally responsible for a cost change because of changes in output of the subject product or service, but only those activities.

Investment and other fixed costs ordinarily are not considered in a base-type marginal cost study. (Chapters 6 and 7 discuss situations where it is necessary to include all or a part of fixed costs.)

Step 8. The Marginal Cost Calculations

Theory defines marginal cost as the change in total costs resulting from a change in output. Taken literally, this definition would require that all variable costs, plus fixed costs, be compared in before-and-after totals. This is done in Step 9, but it may be convenient (as well as a valuable check) to focus first only on the variable costs that have been selected as being causally responsible for the cost change. The procedure first calculates per unit cost changes and then total cost changes for these selected variable costs, as independent but related calculations.

To illustrate, assume that the condition to be analyzed is the production of 100,000 additional units of the subject product.

The Per Unit of Product Basis

Working with the company's engineers, the composition of the product and its costs per unit are estimated to be as follows for future production:

	Marginal cost per additional unit (in cents)
Steel	9.5
Fabricated parts	14.0
Packaging	0.5
Worker's pay	24.0
Energy usage	1.0
Billing expense	0.5
Plant operations and maintenance	0.5
Total marginal costs per unit	50.0

This total marginal cost per unit suggests that the increase in cost for 100,000 additional units would be $50,000.

The Total Variable Cost Basis

Independently, the company's accounting and budget staff are asked to estimate the selected variable costs as they are with present production and as they would be if production were to be increased by 100,000 units. Their figures are:

	Present production	Increased production
Purchasing department	$2,200,000	$2,223,000
Shipping department	50,000	51,000
Billing department	40,000	40,500
Energy bills	60,000	61,000
Plant operations and maintenance	30,000	30,500
Wages	2,620,000	2,644,000
Total production costs	$5,000,000	$5,050,000

The above before and after costs show the same increase of $50,000 as was indicated by the per unit calculation. Thus the two methods check, although not precisely for every item. (This symmetry in results is, of course, no accident. The tables were framed to be so.)

In most actual cases the results of the two methods cannot be expected to correspond so closely. It is no cause for alarm if they are not exactly the same, but the analyst must go back to the drawing boards if the difference is large.

Both methods should be calculated when it is possible to do so. Reliance on only one method or the other can lead to a substantial unnoticed error in the results.

Step 9. The Total Cost Calculation

Other than to comply with theory, it is probably not absolutely essential that the marginal cost study include a showing of all costs, fixed and variable, on a before-and-after basis. The change in these total costs should be the same as the change in the impacted variable costs derived from Step 8.

This additional step is helpful because it provides a further check on the prior results, and puts the output change into the context of the enterprise's overall operations.

A total cost showing is particularly valuable when the study involves public policy issues, as is the case in the school voucher study of chapter 5. Presenting only the specific variable costs that change with output changes is likely to give an incomplete and possibly misleading picture to observers who are not familiar with the base technique.

4. Achieving Economic Efficiency in Regulated Pricing

as Framed by Alfred E. Kahn

Kahn's two-volume work, *The Economics of Regulation* (1970–71),[1] inspired serious consideration throughout the United States of marginal cost pricing theory as a regulatory basis for utility rate setting, and led to the adoption of the theory as a formal standard for pricing in many states, including California.

The first section of this chapter quotes the *Economics* as it discusses "Economic Efficiency and Marginal Cost." These quotes are seminal statements of microeconomic theory and sketch key requisites for the achievement of economic efficiency by means of marginal cost pricing.

Kahn's later refinements of theory, which bear upon matters related to the Summers challenge, are captured in the sequence in which they appeared in several sources in the later sections of this chapter.

The chapter closes with notes from Kahn's latest book, *Letting Go*, which focuses on many issues coming to the fore in the New Economy.

To capture the flavor of Kahn's thoughts, and to avoid misinterpretations of his pricing prescriptions, extensive use is made of direct quotations.

Chapter 4 is supplemented by an appendix, "Pre-Kahn Theory," which sketches marginal cost theory as it existed prior to the *Economics*.

The *Economics* on Economic Efficiency and Marginal Cost

Beginning Thoughts

Kahn states: ". . . traditional theory provides guiding *principles*: these define the goal of economic efficiency and provide rules for achieving it . . ." (vii). These are rules "inherent in the normative model of the competitive market system" (19) and in "a normative theory of public policy" (vii).

Ideal results (optimality) will see ". . . the use of society's limited resources in such a way as to maximize consumer satisfactions" (17). The regulatory test should be ". . . the efficiency with which [prices, or in utility terminology, rates] make use of society's resources . . ." (29).

"Economic efficiency calls for a uniform price to all buyers of an identical service at any given time (unless there can be perfect price discrimination . . .)" (71, footnote 19).

"*Perfect price discrimination* involves fashioning charges according to what each unit of traffic will bear," its basis being "differences not in cost but in demand . . . not achievable in actual practice" (132).

"The *entire justification* for marginal cost pricing lies in the elasticity of demand—the fact that customers will buy more or less than the optimum amount if price is lower or higher than marginal cost. More *satisfactions* are conferred on buyers than are taken away from sellers when prices are reduced to marginal cost; producers can be spared losses greater than the buyer *satisfactions* sacrificed if prices that are below marginal costs are raised to that level" (131).

An Interpretation

1. "Economic efficiency" is an alternative term for the utilization of resources so as to "maximize consumer satisfactions." As a principle, the maximization of consumer satisfactions (optimality) is the gauge of economic efficiency.

Thus, economic efficiency rests upon the yardstick of consumer satisfactions.

2. Because resources are finite and society's capacity to produce is limited, the *choice* to produce a given product or service necessarily means that less of other products or services can be produced. The cost of a given item, therefore, can be defined as consisting of the other items

sacrificed in order to produce the given item. Restating this proposition in terms of consumer satisfactions, the cost of producing a given product or service is *opportunity cost*, the consumer satisfactions that must be forgone by reason of choosing the given product or service over alternatives.

This flow of definitional logic seems to suggest that satisfactions gained from a produced product or service should equal satisfactions forgone; and that the solution to the equation requires a *yardstick* of consumer satisfactions gained or forgone.

3. If consumers make their "independent purchase decisions" on the basis of such a yardstick, "they will . . . guide our scarce resources into those lines of production that yield more satisfactions than all available alternatives—which means that total satisfactions will be maximized" (66). In other words, *economic efficiency, which is a proxy term for the maximization of consumer satisfactions*, will have been achieved.

Marginal Cost Theory

Kahn begins with the statement that microeconomic theory (expressed under the condition of *ceteris paribus* "all other things remaining equal") observes or predicts that "under pure competition price will be set at marginal cost" (16).

Normative (welfare) Microeconomics (56)

> Microeconomics . . . is interested first and foremost in the determination of individual prices. Its normative models also include certain notions about the appropriate relation between an industry's average prices or total revenues on the one hand and its average or total costs on the other; but that optimum is conceived to be the result or *end product* of a competitive process that operates directly and in the first instance in individual markets, in the fixing of individual prices.[87]
>
> With respect to those individual markets, the rules of microeconomics are in principle simple and grounded in objective facts: *subject to important qualifications* that we shall elaborate at a later point, prices should be equated to marginal costs. In this scheme, there is no room for separate considerations of "fairness." Or, to put it another way, fairness is defined in strictly economic terms: those prices are fair that are equal to marginal costs, those unfair that are not equal.

---

87. These comments may seem arbitrarily to suggest that short-run equilibrium is somehow more important than long-run, and in so doing to reflect the

essentially static character of traditional economic theory, or its tendency simply to assume mobility of resources sufficient to ensure the achievement of long-run equilibrium. In a dynamic world and in the presence of resource immobilities, competition sufficiently pure to hold prices constantly at short-run marginal cost may prove destructive and violently unstable; and much of the pricing in impurely competitive or oligopolistic markets can often be understood as seeking to achieve the long-run competitive result—which in a perfectly competitive market could safely be left to instantaneous inflows and outflows of labor and capital—at the possible expense of the constant equation of price with short-run marginal cost. The student of industrial organization may be as much concerned with the process that holds an industry's total profits, averaged over some period of time, at the competitive level as that its individual prices be instantaneously equated with short-term marginal cost.

The fact remains that the welfare ideal is constructed on the basis of the equation of price to marginal cost in individual markets and in the short-run. That is where the process starts. Departures from that standard must be individually justified.

The Rationale (and Related Terms)

The Conclusion

"The central policy prescription of microeconomics is the equation of price and marginal cost" (65).

Terms (65–66)

Marginal Cost is the cost of producing one more unit; it can equally be envisaged as the cost that would be saved by producing one less unit. Looking at the first way, it may be termed incremental cost—the added cost of (a small amount of) incremental output. Observed in the second way, it is synonymous with avoidable cost—the cost that would be saved by (slightly) reducing output. (Although these three terms are often used synonymously, marginal cost, strictly speaking, refers to the additional cost of supplying a single, infinitesimally small additional unit, while 'incremental' and 'avoidable' are sometimes used to refer to the average additional cost of a finite and possibly a large change in production or sales.)

The Question, Part I (66)

"Why does the economist argue that, ideally, *every buyer* ought to pay a price equal to the cost of supplying one incremental unit?"

The Answer

At any given time, every economy has a fixed bundle of productive resources, a finite total potential productive capacity. Or course, that total can grow over time; but at any given time the basic economic problem is to make the best or most efficient use of that limited capacity. The basic economic problem, in short, is the problem of choice. A decision to produce more of any one good or service is, in these circumstances, *ipso facto* a decision to produce less of all other goods and services taken as a bunch. It follows that the cost to society of producing anything consists, really, in the other things that must be sacrificed in order to produce it: in the last analysis, *"cost" is opportunity cost—the alternatives that must be foregone.* In our economy, we leave the final decision about what shall be produced and what not to the voluntary decisions of purchasers,[11] guided by prices on the one hand and their own wants or preferences on the other.

If consumers are to make the choices that will yield them the greatest possible satisfaction from society's limited aggregate productive capacity, the prices that they pay for the various goods and services available to them must accurately reflect their respective opportunity costs; only then will buyers be judging, in deciding what to buy and what not, whether the satisfaction they get from the purchase of any particular product is worth the sacrifice of other goods and services that its production entails. If their judgments are correctly informed in this way, they will, by their independent purchase decisions, guide our scarce resources into those lines of production that yield more satisfaction than all available alternatives—which means that total satisfaction will be maximized.

---

11. We briefly summarize the familiar rationalization of a market system, in which the consumer is supposed to be sovereign. How "voluntary," or "free" consumer decisions actually are in any such economy is an interesting and important question. To the extent that an economic system influences consumer tastes, it is no longer possible for an economist to describe its functioning as "optimal" or "efficient" on the ground that it gives consumers what they want, since the system itself helps determine what they want.

The Question, Part II (66–67)

"But why does economic efficiency require prices equal to marginal, instead of, for example, average total costs?"

The Answer

The reason is that the demand for all goods and services is in some degree, at some point, responsive to price. Then, if consumers are to decide intelligently whether to take somewhat more or somewhat less of any particular item, the price they have to pay for it (and the prices of all other goods and services with which they compare it) must reflect the cost of supplying somewhat more or somewhat less—in short, marginal opportunity cost. If buyers are charged more than marginal cost for a particular commodity, for example because the seller has monopoly power, they will buy less than the optimum quantity; consumers who would willingly have had society allocate to its production the incremental resources required, willingly sacrificing the alternative goods and services that those resources could have produced, will refrain from making those additional purchases because the price to them exaggerates the sacrifices. Conversely, if price is below incremental costs, perhaps because the suppliers are being subsidized, production of the products in question will be higher (and of all other products taken together lower) than it ought to be: society is sacrificing more of other goods and services to produce the additional quantities of the subsidized service than customers would willingly have authorized, had the price to them fully reflected that marginal opportunity cost.

The corollary of the social rule that price should equal marginal cost is the rule of thumb for the businessman—it pays him to continue to produce and sell as long as his incremental revenues cover his incremental costs. Since under pure competition incremental revenues to the businessman are simply the market price times the additional quantities sold, we have the elementary proposition that under pure competition businessmen will increase production and sales up to the point where their marginal costs are equated to price. Therefore, competitive behavior assures the equation of price and marginal cost that is required if free consumer choices are to result in the optimum allocation of resources.

A Recapitulation

The nexis of the translation of marginal costs (marginal opportunity costs) into prices is about as follows.

(i) Demand is responsive to price (in some degree, at some point) (66). Then, if consumers "are to decide intelligently whether to take somewhat *more* or somewhat *less* of any particular item, the price they have to pay for it . . . must reflect the cost of supplying somewhat more or somewhat less [of other items]—in short, *marginal* opportunity cost" (66).

"If buyers are charged more than marginal cost . . . they will buy less than the optimum quantity . . . conversely, if price is below incremental costs . . . production of the products in question will be higher (and of all other products taken together lower) than it ought to be" (66–67).

(ii) This proposition correlates with the businessman's rule of thumb that ". . . under pure competition businessmen will increase production and sales up to the point where their marginal costs are equated to price. Therefore, competitive behavior assures that equation of price and marginal cost that is required if free consumer choices are to result in the optimum allocation of resources" (67).

The rationale for both (i) and (ii) above rests upon the link between prices in the actual economy and prices as would prevail under *the condition of pure competition.*

The Corollaries (69)

There are two corollaries of the marginal cost pricing principle:

1. Prices must reflect all the (marginal) costs of production and consumption not only those borne directly by the transacting parties, but also those that may be foisted on outsiders. (A familiar case of an external cost is the air or stream pollution that may be caused by a particular production process or a particular act of consumption. If it is not borne by the responsible party, his marginal cost will understate the true opportunity cost of the transaction in question—the true sacrifice involved in making it possible—and the result will be overproduction of the good or service in question.) All the social benefits of particular acts of production or consumption must similarly accrue to or otherwise be brought to bear in (positively) influencing the decisions of the buyers, who alone will determine whether the production is undertaken.

2. The rule does not necessarily produce optimal results if it is applied only partially: it does not necessarily provide a correct guide for pricing in individual markets or industries if it is not being followed uniformly throughout the economy. If, for example, the price of good *A* is held above marginal cost, perhaps by monopoly or by disproportionately heavy taxation, then it may produce a worse instead of a better allocation of resources to push the price of its substitute, *B*, down to marginal cost. This *"problem of the second best"* is obviously a very

serious one in an economy shot through with imperfections of competition, monopoly power, and government taxes and subsidies, causing all prices to diverge in varying directions and degrees from marginal costs. The "first best" solution, in the foregoing example, would be to reduce the prices of both *A* and *B* (and of all other goods and services in the economy) to marginal costs; the "second best" *might* be to keep the price of *B* above its marginal cost, perhaps by means of an excise tax, in order to avoid distorting buyers' choices between it and *A*.[17]

---

17. On the other hand one cannot be certain, strictly speaking, that this is the proper solution without taking into account all other distortions in the economy as well. . . . The existence of pervasive imperfections in the economy greatly complicates the problem of efficient pricing. (70)

Kahn's two corollaries represent substantial modification of the economic rationale: (1) marginal costs must include *externalities*; and (2) optimal results occur only if marginal costs are *followed uniformly throughout the economy.*

The Qualifications (67–68)

It is impossible here to provide an adequate survey of all the assumptions, definitions, and value judgments implicit in the foregoing sketchy summary, or of all qualifications to which *the marginal cost equals price rule* must be subjected. Many will be introduced, where appropriate, as we go along: recall . . . that marginal cost is (only) the place to *begin*. But we must point out at once that the allocation of resources that the rule produces can be described as *"optimal"* only on the basis of *two essentially unprovable assumptions or value judgments*: that the "best" economy is the one that gives consumers what they individually want; and that income is either distributed optimally or can best be redistributed without departing from marginal cost pricing.

1. One need accept the allocation of resources the rule produces in a market economy only to the extent that one approves of the choices consumers make or would make. The economist has no scientific basis for objecting if, instead, society decides to improve on the result, either by trying to influence consumer choices (for example by education or by taxing or prohibiting sale of goods whose consumptions it wishes to discourage) or by subsidizing the production of goods it thinks would otherwise be consumed in inadequate quantities. The question of what is the

best measure or definition of social welfare, which it is the function of the economy to serve, is a political or philosophical, not an economic, one. Economics as such is the science of means, not ends.

2. One need accept the result as optimal only if one is willing to place a similar evaluation on the distribution of income—either the preexisting distribution of income, which decides how many dollar votes each buyer has in deciding what to order the economy to produce, or the distribution of income that results from equating price to marginal cost.[14]

---

14. For example, equating price to marginal costs produces economic rents—scarcity returns to nonreproducible factors of production of super-marginal quality.

Fully Distributed Costs

". . . the basic defect of fully distributed costs as a basis for [utility] ratemaking is that they do not necessarily measure marginal cost responsibility *in a causal sense*. They do not measure by what amount costs would be increased if additional quantities of any particular service were taken, or by what amount costs would be reduced if the service were correspondingly curtailed. They are average costs. . ." (151).

Problems of Defining Marginal Cost

The Time Perspective (71)

When the competitive model prescribes prices equated to marginal costs, does it mean the incremental short-run, variable cost of operating existing capacity or intermediate-run cost, which will include also the prospectively mounting costs of repair, maintenance and operation or the long-run costs of ultimately renewing, replacing or adding to capacity?

. . . there is no single answer. But the economic principles are clear cut. They are two.

(1) . . . the criterion . . . is *causal responsibility* . . . *only* such additional [costs], but also *all* such, as are imposed on the economy by the provision of one additional unit.

(2) . . . it is the short-run marginal cost to which price should at any given time—*hence always*—be equated, because it is short-run marginal cost that reflects the *social opportunity cost* of providing the additional unit that buyers are at any given time trying to decide whether to buy.

Short-run marginal cost "is simply the change in *total variable cost* caused by producing an additional unit . . . [These are costs which] vary with output (regardless of when they are actually felt or give rise to additional cash outlays] . . . [Depreciation *which is a function of use*] is a variable cost [and should be included]. . . . [However] to the extent that maintenance, depreciation, cost of capital, and various other overhead expenses are *not* a function of use, they do not belong in short-run marginal cost or, as such, in the ideal price" (71–72).

"*In long-run competitive equilibrium, price will be at precisely the point . . . where short-run marginal costs and average total costs are equal*" (74, n. 25).

The Incremental Block of Output

". . . the proper size of the incremental unit of output depends on the perspective of the decision under consideration" (76). Drawing analogies from the airlines, Kahn notes that the block could range from carrying an extra passenger on an unfilled flight (in which case the marginal cost "would be practically zero") to regular service between a pair of cities. "The larger the incremental unit of service under consideration, the more costs become variable" (75).

Practicality vs. Theory

". . . the economically efficient price . . . is set at the short-run marginal cost (SRMC) of the smallest possible additional unit of sale" (83). But, typically this is not practicable. Marginal costs will vary from one moment to the next, and their calculation is often "infeasible or prohibitively expensive" (83–84).

> . . . the practically-achievable version of SRMC pricing is often likely to be pricing at *average* variable costs (AVC), themselves averaged over some period of time in the past and assumed to remain constant over some period in the future—until there occurs some clear, discrete shift caused by an event such as a change in wage rates. But since short-term AVC (in contrast with SRMC) are never as large as average total costs . . . , universal adoption of this type of pricing is infeasible if sellers are to cover total costs, including (as always) a minimum required return on investment. This in turn produces a strong tendency in industry to price on a "full cost" basis—usually computed at AVC (really *average* AVC over some

period of time) plus some percentage mark-up judged sufficient to cover total costs on the average over some time period—a far cry, indeed, from marginal cost pricing (84). SRMC can be above or below ATC (average *total* cost) . . . [49] . . . the practically achievable benchmark for efficient pricing is more likely to be a type of *average long-run incremental cost*, computed for a large, expected incremental block of sales, instead of SRMC, estimated for a single additional sale. This long-run incremental cost (which we shall loosely refer to as *long-run marginal cost* as well) would be based on (1) the average incremental variable costs of those added sales and (2) estimated additional capital costs per unit, for the additional capacity that will have to be constructed if sales at that price are expected to continue over time or to grow. Both of these components would be estimated as averages over some period of years extending into the future. (84–85)

Long-run marginal costs are likely to be the preferred criterion also in competitive situations [as well as where there is a prevalence of common costs]. Permitting rate reductions to a lower level of SRMC, which would prove to be unremunerative if the business thus attracted were to continue over time, might constitute predatory competition—driving out of business rivals whose *long-run* costs of production might well be lower than those of the price-cutter. (85)

---

49. If SRMC pricing did not cover ATC over time, capital would eventually be withdrawn and new capital, needed to meet the rising demand, repelled, until a recovering demand, moving up along a steeply rising MC curve, pushed prices up high enough and held them there long enough to attract new capital into the industry—with the possibility of a return of depressed prices with any temporary reemergence of excess capacity. (85)

Professor Kahn recognizes that the immediately foregoing tempers "principle with practicality" (83). Having stated, as quoted earlier, that ". . . it is the short-run marginal cost [SRMC] to which price should at any given time—*hence always*—be equated . . ." (71) he has changed position to substitute long-run marginal cost (which he defines as "a type of average long-run incremental cost" (85). Professor Kahn summarizes:

The limitations of trying to base prices solely on SRMC may be stated more generally. The theory of efficient pricing that we sketched earlier in this chapter is a static theory.[2] It describes the conditions for optimum choosing, given some preexisting technology and pattern of consumer desires. It describes the optimum, equilibrium outcome that will prevail after all adjustments have been made to those two fundamental determinants of supply and demand functions. It makes no calculation of the costs or likelihood of achieving that result in a dynamic economy, in which demand and costs are constantly changing. Or, alternatively, it may be said to describe *how that result will be achieved effortlessly, costlessly, and instantaneously under perfect competition*—where buyers and sellers of every good and service are infinitely numerous, have perfect knowledge and foresight and act rationally on it and where resources are perfectly mobile and fully employed. But obviously these conditions do not and cannot prevail in the real world. Only, then, if we can compare the efficiency gains of each proposed movement toward SRMC pricing, on the one hand, with its possible costs and drawbacks in a world of imperfect competition, knowledge, rationality, and resource mobility can we decide whether that move is indeed optimal even in purely economic terms. We have just suggested several reasons why it might not always be optimal. (86)

This list of considerations is by no means exhaustive. Since the best probable compromise of offsetting considerations will clearly vary from one pricing context to another, it is impossible to set forth an integrated, general set of conclusions. Instead what we have is really a set of hypotheses, of relevant considerations. (86)

Matching Marginal and Total Costs

Where marginal costs (MC) of the several classes of utility service are not sufficient to result in necessary aggregate avenues, Kahn notes that: "According to one standard of welfare economics, the prices of the various services should be marked up above MC in inverse proportion to their elasticities of demand" (144). (This is often referred to as the "inverse elasticity" rule or "Ramsey pricing.") Kahn observes that this approach has the effect of favoring elastic demand customers over inelastic demand customers and that ". . . economics can supply no common denominator for comparing or adding up the *psychic satisfactions*" (145) of the two categories of customers. Kahn concludes:

> Mainly for this reason—and also because of the difficulty of measuring demand elasticities—some economists have opposed the use of price discrimination in public utility rate making, advocating instead that the long-run marginal costs of as many classes of service as possible be identified and rates be set uniformly above those respective costs by whatever percentage [is] required to bring in the necessary aggregate revenues. That is, instead of the various rates being set discriminatorily at varying percentages of marginal costs, in (inverse) dependence on the respective

elasticities of demand, the price to marginal cost ratios would be constant for all classes of service. (145)

(This is referred to as the "equal percentage of marginal cost" (EPMC) rule, which has been adopted by the California Public Utilities Commission (CPUC).)

In this respect, it is pertinent to note that Kahn earlier has declared: ". . . charging any customer more or less than the marginal cost of serving him violates the dictates of economic efficiency . . ." (123).

Qualifications to the Theory

Qualifications

In many respects, Kahn's concluding chapter of his Volume I (chapter 7) is the most extraordinary, and perhaps also the most noteworthy. It is here that Kahn qualifies—one might say nullifies—much of the economic dogma previously presented as "principles of economically efficient public utility pricing."

Justice cannot be done to this chapter without reproducing it in full. It is recommended that the reader do just that by referring to the actual text. Limited space makes it necessary to be satisfied with a few key points, while apologizing for the omission of others that may be as or more important.

> The task of translating these principles into actual price schedules is so extraordinarily difficult that it is entirely possible to accept their validity while at the same time concluding that the task of following them is an impossible one. Few would go as far as to abandon the effort entirely. But all would point out, and correctly so, that even the most sophisticated and conscientious effort to apply these principles inevitably involves *large doses of subjective judgment* and, at the very best, *can achieve only the roughest possible approximation of the desired results*. The uncertainty of the resulting estimates and the impossibility of devising and enforcing rate structures that fully embody them counsel a rounding of the edges, a tempering of the principles themselves. Such a tempering is not necessarily objectionable even on purely economic grounds: as we have already pointed out, the economic costs of ascertaining and enforcing economically efficient rates, in particular circumstances, can well outweigh the efficiency advantages that such rates are supposed to achieve. (182)

The difficulty of estimating marginal cost . . . [including estimating demand elasticity and future costs]. (183)

. . . the costs and benefits [of externalities] must somehow be brought to bear on the powers of deciding how much shall be produced, how, and by whom. (183) Externalities are ubiquitous, [particularly for utilities].

. . . if prices in the economy generally are not uniformly set at social marginal cost, . . . then the efficient price for the utility service must no longer necessarily be set at marginal cost either. . . . Thus the problem of "*Second-best*: what prices will produce the efficient allocation of resources in a world of imperfect competition and differential taxes and subsidies." (183)

Continuing on the "second best" problem of "translating principle into policy:"

Deviations *anywhere* else in the economy from optimal pricing and resource allocation make it impossible to conclude *as a general proposition* that application in any single sector of the normative rules that we have been developing will be desirable. No single policy decision can be determined to be optimal except on the basis of a general equilibrium analysis of the situation in the entire economy, which takes into account all the ways in which that equilibrium will be altered by the adoption of any particular policy for any particular part of the economy—manifestly an impossible task. (195)

This general proposition means that, as a matter of pure economics, adoption of any particular economic policy on the basis of the rules we have expounded could well end up doing more harm than good in practice. But the observation applies equally to the policy of having *no* policy. (196)

. . .

. . . here, as elsewhere, there is no substitute for judgment when one comes to the job of applying our principles. . . (196)

. . . the principal virtue of setting rates at marginal cost is the virtue of competition; it exerts the maximum pressure on competitors to improve their own efficiency and service offerings. (198)

In the "Conclusion" of this chapter, Professor Kahn is philosophical.

In view of the pervasive uncertainties with respect to the measurement of marginal costs and elasticities of demand, certain dangers are introduced by following the economic principles we have enunciated . . . (198)

But any system of pricing involves the exercise of judgment. The question is whether that judgment should be employed in order best to apply economically efficient principles or irrational principles.[39]

39. An approximation, even one subject to a wide margin of error, to the correct answer is better than the wrong answer worked out to seven decimal places. (199)

It is regrettable that many disciples of Kahn have painted the "marginal cost = economic efficiency" doctrine so dogmatically. It is rare indeed for the protagonist-practitioners to admit to any imperfections of their interpretations of the doctrine as they pursue their search for the Golden Grail.

The Objective Restated (Lowest Cost)

Under the heading, "The Central Role of Long-run Marginal Costs," Kahn states the marginal cost objective in different terms—achieving the lowest possible cost for consumers.

> Apart from possible noneconomic considerations, society's interest is in having transportation, energy, or communications provided *at the lowest possible cost*, with due allowance for possible differences in the quality of services supplied or the costs imposed on the users. And economic efficiency requires, additionally, that no business be turned away that covers the cost to society of providing that service. These basic goals are served by permitting rates to be set at long-run marginal costs. The consequence will be that, after consumers have made allowance in their choices for possible differences in the quality of the service, the competing company with the lowest long-run marginal costs will get the business; and the services will thus be provided by those companies that, in so doing, will impose the minimum opportunity costs on the economy at large. (160–61)

At a different point, he adds: "Reducing rates to marginal costs is exactly the way in which competition is supposed to achieve an efficient allocation of business at the primary level" (175) and, "The presence of competition [increases] the desirability of setting the lower limit at long-run instead of short-run marginal costs" (176).

Pure (Perfect) Competition

Since the 1930s, dating from the writings of Joan Robinson and Edward Hastings Chamberlin, economists have formally recognized that the model of pure competition is the rare exception not the norm.

Professor Kahn, of course, is fully aware of this. He refers to "theoretically perfect but practically unachievable competition," (II, 241) and declares "all competition is imperfect . . ." (II, 329).

In comments dated December 23, 1996, directed toward ". . . the restrictive conditions of a perfectly competitive market at equilibrium," the Office of Ratepayer Advocates of the California PUC delineates the classic economic model of pure (or perfect) competition as follows:

The four conditions of perfect competition are:

1. The products are identical across sellers.
2. Each buyer or seller is sufficiently small relative to the market that he or she cannot influence the product price.
3. All resources are completely mobile.
4. Consumers, firms, and resource owners have perfect knowledge of economic and technological data.

The Pubic Utilities Fortnightly Articles, 1978

After his chairmanship of the New York PUC (1974 to early 1977), Kahn become chairman of the Civil Aeronautics Board in June 1977. Early in the next year he wrote three articles, published in *Public Utilities Fortnightly*, which recounted his views as an economist-turned-regulator. His emphasis throughout the three articles was on the application of economic principles to utility rate regulation.

January 5, 1978, "Can an Economist Find Happiness Setting Public Utility Rates?"

Kahn answered the question posed in the topic of this first article with an emphatic "yes." He declared that his purpose in writing the articles was "to demonstrate by concrete examples the ubiquitous applicability of simple economic principles in the real world . . . [especially] application of economic theory [to] rates." But, he pointed out, "economics has much more to contribute to regulatory policy than the mere equation of price to marginal cost."

The Future

Kahn emphasized the importance of the future: "the costs which are reflected in rates [should be] reasonably representative of the circumstances in the [future] period during which the rates will be in effect. . . ."

Sunk Costs

More than twenty years before sunk costs become the pressing issue it is today as utility restructuring progresses, and as the Summers challenge is being considered, Kahn recognized its looming importance:

> Must a public utility regulator raise rates in order to permit companies the full recovery of sunk costs, when, as any economist knows, sunk costs are bygones that ought to be ignored? There is no easy answer. Commissions have limited gross returns in periods of sharply increasing demand, when a competitive market would have permitted more; they are therefore hard put to justify refusing to recognize requests for the continuous recovery of those costs on incompletely depreciated plant in periods when its utilization is declining. Investors will obviously think twice about supplying new capital to companies regulated by a commission that shows a tendency to ignore the costs associated with infusions of capital in the past. But the only economic justification for a return on sunk investment is to reflect the incremental costs of new production in order on the one hand to ration consumption and on the other to attract needed capital.

He then lays down the principle he feels should be followed:

> The resources that we irretrievably used yesterday can no longer be conserved today: That is the reason for the economist's indifference to sunk cost. It follows that the only costs that are relevant for efficient resource utilization and conservation are the costs that are current at the time purchase decisions are made. Anything, therefore, that brings the total revenues a company is permitted to collect closer to current costs is a step in the direction of giving consumers price signals reflecting the sacrifices society is making in supplying them or would save if they abstained from purchasing.

Kahn was careful to point out that the function of rate increases "is not to recover sunk costs, but to attract new capital," observing that "when new capital needs are great, increases have to be correspondingly generous; where needs are slight, they can be correspondingly so."

Deregulation

One of the most interesting parts of this article, looked at some twenty years later, is Kahn's remark that when capital requirements for new projects are sufficiently large (as they were for a then-proposed $8 billion Alaskan natural gas pipeline), he "would counsel total deregulation of the permitted rate of return." This, of course, would amount to deregulation of the overall revenue ceiling, unheard of at the time.

January 19, 1978, "Applications of Economics to Utility Rate Structures"

In this second article, Kahn amplifies on subjects he has mentioned earlier.

Marginal Costs: Short-Run or Long-Run?[3]

"In equilibrium, the two are equal. . . . In the frictionless world of perfect knowledge, resource mobility and rational responses, prices should, of course, be based on the former. These are a number of reasons why it might be preferable, however, to base rates on long-run incremental costs (LRIC)."

Long-Run Incremental Cost Defined

Long-run incremental cost (LRIC)[4] is "the amount by which costs will differ, after a span of time sufficiently long for the system planners to adapt the supply system to the change, by virtue of taking on some specified incremental block of sales on a continuing basis . . . *LRIC pricing involves an explicit incorporation of capital charges in price*" (Emphasis added).

Long-Run Incremental Cost Advantages

In addition to greater stability and continuity in rates, LRIC gives consumers making investment decisions "the best signals of what rates will be over the life of that equipment."

The Merging of Short Run and Long Run

The following quotation is of great importance to theory, including its references to externalities and proxies.

> In any event, short-run marginal cost (SRMC) pricing may merge into LRIC in practice, once one recognizes that one important component of (short-run) variable costs properly attributable to increments in

consumption—a component whose dimensions vary depending upon the timing of that incremental demand in relation to the system peak—is the increased congestion, or the increased probability of a system being unable to satisfy all demands placed upon it (sometimes termed marginal curtailment costs), and the consequent diminished quality of service generally that it causes. These external costs are extremely difficult to measure directly. The most convenient surrogate is the cost of the additional capacity that would have to be installed in order to hold the probability of such a decline in quality of service at its previous level. In this way, a capacity charge—i.e., a direct contribution to fixed costs—gets incorporated into even an SRMC-based price, by proxy.

February 2, 1978, "The Economics of Regulation: Externalities and Institutional Issues"

The publisher describes this third and last article of the series as a discussion of "the implications and treatment of problems stemming from economic 'imperfections,' sometimes requiring 'second best' solutions."

Second Best

The Problem. Marginal cost pricing requires "considering the problem of second best—the problem that prices of other goods and services may not be at their respective marginal costs, in which event pricing electricity or gas or water or anything else at its marginal cost may actually be economically inefficient."

The Question. Does this problem counsel "in favor or against moving to marginal cost-based electric rates?"

The Solution. "Purely deductive reasoning" does not yield an answer. Rather,

> What is required is an examination of how other, most directly pertinent prices in the economy do actually stand relative to their marginal costs. These would be the prices of goods and services for which electricity is a substitute; with which electricity is used, as a complement; in whose supply electricity is an input; and which themselves constitute inputs in the production and delivery of electricity.

He adds this warning, as an additional reason for marginal cost pricing:

> A failure to get the price of electricity up correspondingly will therefore discourage economically sound investments in these energy-conserving

devices and practices, and result in uneconomic consumption of energy. And this, of course, is the fundamental case for marginal cost pricing in the first place.

. . .

In a first-best world, prices would include the residual (marginal) external costs as well. But it must be recognized that such costs thoroughly pervade a second-best world, and there is, so far as I can see, no reason to assume, a priori, that they bulk larger inside the public utility arena than outside in which event the principle of second best counsels against trying to incorporate them in the prices we set.

On Regulation

The following is uniquely pertinent as utility restricting and deregulation movements enter into the twenty-first century: "Regulated monopoly is a very imperfect institution, and wherever the processes of the market can be substituted, they should be."

The Richard T. Ely Lecture, 1978[5]

In August 1978, Kahn delivered the Richard T. Ely lecture before the American Economic Association. Its subject was "Application of Economics to an Imperfect World," and, as the subject suggests, reflects Kahn's struggles to adapt neoclassical microeconomics, patterned on the assumption of perfect competition, to the real economy in which perfect competition is rare or nonexistent. At the time of this lecture, Kahn was chairman of the Civil Aeronautics Board (CAB). He had emerged from academe as Robert Julius Thorne Professor of Economics at Cornell University to become chairman of the New York State Public Utilities Commission (NYSPUC), from which he went to the CAB. In both jobs he dealt with a monopolistic and highly regulated business environment—quite the opposite of laissez-faire.[6]

In 1978, Kahn saw his New York Commission and CAB experiences as affording "almost unlimited opportunity for the application of simple micro-economic principles to the real world" (1). He remains faithful to these principles, while recognizing the difficulties of implementation:

The applicable principles are easy to characterize: that economic efficiency calls for prices equated to marginal social opportunity costs; and that, whenever it is technologically feasible, competition is the best institutional mechanism for achieving that result, as well as for minimizing X-inefficiency and ensuring the optimum rate of innovation . . .

But the process of applying these principles—even of simply getting out of the way—has been far from simple . . . the world to which [the economist-regulator] would apply his principles is excruciatingly imperfect and resistant; and the compass he needs is one that would help him thread his way through the thickets of second best. The really challenging job is deciding not what the ultimate economically rational equilibrium should look like, but what is economically rational in an irrational world, and how best to get from here to there.

[The economist-regulator is offered] an irresistible opportunity to use price—typically very imprecisely and inefficiently—as an instrument for the redistribution of income. (1)

The *Yale Journal on Regulation* Article, 1987[7]

In this long article on "Current Issues in Telecommunications Regulation: Pricing," Kahn, joined by William B. Shew, extends his thoughts on micro pricing theory and practice. While the main concerns of the article are local and long distance telephone rates, its stated principles and observations are equally applicable to costing and pricing in the economy at large.

Marginal Costs

The Outlook

Economically efficient pricing looks not to the past—not to how we got where we are—but to the future; efficiency requires that prices tell customers what incremental resources society will use if they take more of the good or service in question, what resources society will save if they consume less of it. (224)

The Number

. . . the straightforward economic principle [is] that marginal cost is not a unique number but a functional relation between output and cost, whose value will vary from one part of an industry's supply function to another. The value that is relevant for efficient pricing will be determined by the level and elasticity of demand at various prices. (224, footnote 80)

Sunk Costs (Capital Fixed Costs) in Relation to Short-Run Marginal Cost and Long-Run Incremental Cost

There is no truism in economics more elementary than that sunk costs are to be ignored in deciding how best to use the resources that are available to us today and that will be available in the future. This truism does not mean that first-best efficiency ignores fixed costs or makes no provision for their recovery. (225)

. . .

Short-run marginal or incremental costs do not explicitly include [fixed] costs; they include variable costs only. Long-run incremental costs, in contrast, do explicitly include the costs associated with adding capacity. As a matter of pure economic principle, prices should ideally be equated to the former of these, which, properly defined, include opportunity costs (congestion, for example) as well as production costs. Although pricing at short-run marginal cost (SRMC) seems to ignore fixed costs, it is not incompatible with their recovery. On the contrary, SRMC will be above or below average variable costs, depending upon the relationship of production to capacity; so pricing at SRMC will make a contribution to the coverage of capital costs—a contribution that will at times fall short of, and at other times exceed average recovery. (225)

. . .

Moreover, it will ordinarily be more practicable to base utility rates not on short-run, but instead on long-run incremental costs (LRIC). To the extent that in the long run additional consumption or use of a particular service will involve additional investment, the capital costs associated with that investment will be explicitly included in LRIC, and therefore in price. (226)

Allocations and Common Costs

Since regulators and economists generally accept the desirability of basing the prices [of individual] services on their respective costs, the issues tend to be framed in terms of the proper apportionment of their common costs among them.[8] (194)

[Common costs should not be distributed on the basis of benefits.] Allocations of common costs on the basis of benefits or some other conception of fairness are tautological or telelogical. . . . The only costs which have objective reality are ones that describe a causal relationship between the act of purchase and their incurrence. (206–7)

. . . where a plant provides a number of goods or services in common, economic efficiency requires that it be so designed as to provide them collectively at minimum aggregate cost. The fact that such a design may entail a higher marginal cost and therefore a higher first-best price for one of those services than some other system design is irrelevant. (211–12)

Lumpiness and Spare Capacity

"Telephone companies [like other utilities] build capacity in lumps, so that typically there will be excess capacity. . . . This means that short-run marginal costs . . . are ordinarily below long-run or average costs" (221). Restating the same: "The companies systematically overinvest in capacity, so that the proper marginal cost is typically lower than the long-run marginal and average costs they actually incur" (221).

The presence of spare capacity raises the question of whether the costs of that capacity should be included in the applicable marginal cost. Kahn says "yes," provided it has been installed for the purpose of cost minimization. Economic efficiency requires an efficiently designed system, and spare capacity may be an ingredient of such design (239–40).

Income-Distributional Considerations

Economists universally recognize that moving from one set of prices to another will have different effects on different people, and they accept the relevance of those income-distributional consequences in deciding whether such a change is socially desirable. (253)

. . .

The possibility that more efficient prices will have unfortunate income distributional consequences does not, however, suffice to justify the present economically irrational price structure, and the enormous social welfare losses that it entails. It requires us, rather, to seek ways of forestalling or reversing those consequences that would be less costly than the present system. (254)

The *Electricity Journal* Articles, 1994 and 1998[9]

In 1994 and again in 1998, Kahn wrote at the crossroads of the electric restructuring/deregulation movement. His concerns were somewhat broader and more concentrated on competition than in his earlier articles, but they are still centered on the core issue of the relationship of pricing to economic efficiency.

October 1994, "Can Regulation and Competition Coexist? Solutions to the Stranded Cost Problems and Other Conundra"

> *"I would not be the first or the last economist to predict yesterday more accurately than tomorrow"* (27)

This 1994 article by Kahn shows him to be a good predictor. His foresight was surprisingly correct. But the article is reviewed here from a different perspective. Highlighted is Kahn's struggle to mesh purist marginal cost pricing theory laid down for regulated utilities with the rapid emergence of competitive nonregulated electricity suppliers who are free to price as they see fit. The change in circumstances from monopoly to competition made it expedient to temper purist views, particularly because utility companies were confronted with an overpowering burden of sunk costs (or "stranded investment") accumulated in prior years with regulatory acquiescence, and, in major part, at specific regulatory direction.

These sunk costs, coming into the mid-1980s, had financed "enormous amounts of excess capacity." Marginal costs were "far, far below average costs or average revenue requirements." In the East, "average rates [were] in the eight to twelve cent per kilowatt hour range . . . [while] short-run marginal costs [were] two to three cents and the ability to build new plants and break even [stood] at rates of five cents a kilowatt hour, possibly even lower" (26).

Kahn's thought on this situation is epitomized in the following quote:

If there is one principle in economics that corresponds to the physical law that nature abhors a vacuum, it is that society abhors a great gap between marginal costs and price.[1] (26)

---

1. That principle requires qualification as it applies to the real world: Just as a feather and a brick will fall equally fast in a vacuum—or so they say; I don't really believe it—but not in the real world, so while society ought to abhor equally gaps both positive and negative between marginal costs and price, what it abhors especially are prices far above marginal cost. In general, only economists

and environmentalists experience acute distress when the divergence has the opposite sign. (35)

The Generalized Pricing Solution

These distortions and strains [in pricing by utilities and unregulated firms] can typically be resolved or eliminated only by extending the freedoms symmetrically to all competitors—specifically, giving the local utility companies freedom to price competitively and freedom from the continuing obligation to provide firm backup service without charge to customers who enjoy the freedom to escape the costs of providing that option. (28)

Sunk Cost Recovery Solutions

Kahn again repeats "that economic efficiency would best be served by ignoring sunk costs and freeing utility companies to reduce their rates to marginal costs to the extent necessary to meet competition." He adds that he has "no particular enlightenment" on whether utilities have an "entitlement" to recover sunk costs (30).

But assuming recovery is allowed, he suggests:

". . . an essential to insuring that competition is efficient while also permitting recovery of [generation] stranded costs," is to enable the electric utilities to recover from competitors "the same proportionate contribution above marginal cost as was and remains embedded in their own rates for the business they lose to those competitors, by marking up their charges for access to bottleneck transmission and distribution facilities." (30)

Kahn concludes by stating:

an appropriate charge or mark-up above marginal costs for competitors and incumbent utilities alike is fully compatible with efficient competition between them. (30) [But this] conflicts with first-best economic efficiency because it holds prices above marginal costs and [while consistent with efficient competition among rivals] it prevents competition from achieving its other purpose of driving costs down to marginal costs. (31)
. . . excess capacity could be exploited by promoting sales of power at rates closer to marginal costs. (31)
. . . Both equity and first-best economic efficiency require that, just as the price of power itself is driven down to marginal cost, the rates for its

carriage be raised to that same target, to the extent they are at present below it. (32) . . . It could be . . . that mark-ups above regulated transport rates are required for economic efficiency. (31)

The Doctrine in Light of Competition

How do the twain meet—the theory of marginal cost pricing and the reality of competition? Kahn gives his overview.

> Clearly, the efficient price [for transmission and distribution] would be a *marginal* cost. But whether that should be short- or long-run, for small increments or measured in terms of the full marginal cost of providing the service, and how transmission losses, opportunity costs or congestion costs and their variations from one moment to the next and one part of the system to another are to be measured, are all complexities that must be mastered if this possibly promising avenue of reform is to be pursued. (32)
>
> . . .
>
> In situations in which prices set at marginal costs would produce revenues insufficient to give the utility a reasonable opportunity to recover its total revenue requirement—as determined by regulators—all competing sellers should make a proportional contribution to that total, as part of the price they pay for access to ultimate customers via the transmission network and/or by such other devices as may be feasible. As long as the contribution required of competitors is no greater, on a per unit basis, than the contribution reflected in the utility's own charges to the same customers, all sellers will be in a position to compete on the basis of their relative efficiency and, indeed, will be forced to do so. (34)

To You and Me, What Are Sunk Costs?

Kahn seldom reveals in his formal writings the humor for which he is well known. This article contains an exception. He recounts:

> Many years ago, when my wife and I first bought our house on Lake Cayuga, I made a ritual of getting in as many swims as possible during the summer—as soon as the thermometer reached 62 degrees going up and until it hit 62 degrees going down. Asked to explain this compulsion, I responded, only semi-facetiously, that the annual carrying costs of the house were so great, I wanted to spread the fixed costs over the greatest possible number of swims. When challenged by a well-trained former

student: "Didn't you teach us that it's irrational to be influenced by sunk costs?" I responded, I was talking then about other people's sunk costs; these are my sunk costs. While the sunk costs that will be the electric industry's preoccupation for a long time are considerably bigger than the carrying costs of my lake house—and they are its sunk costs, which it is not free to ignore—I had better be very careful about preaching to utility company executives the economic irrelevance—indeed, perversity—of worrying about them. (29–30)

April 1998, "Electric Deregulation: Defining and Ensuring Fair Competition"

Efficiency and Competition

Kahn continues his 1994 contemplation of competition.

Declaring that competitors in the restructured market should prosper or fail on the basis of their "relative efficiency," he defined his term: "The measure of efficiency (holding product quality equal) is incremental costs. Fair competition is competition on the basis of those costs" (40).

Competitive Advantages and Corporate Integration

Advantages that a competitor may bring to the market legitimately, Kahn states, are "economies of scale, scope or experience" which flow from "superior efficiencies." Their exploitation by a competitor promotes consumer welfare; denying them to a competitor in unregulated markets is anticompetitive (41).

Kahn adds, looking directly at the up-to-the-minute issue of corporate integration:

> . . . Competitive advantages arising out of such economies are precisely the kind of efficiency advantages that we expect and want under competition. Integration—extension of a firm's activities to embrace new functions, products or services—is fundamentally a competitive phenomenon, and the efficiency advantages it seeks to exploit are socially beneficent. . . . [Integration is a means of achieving] the benefits of economics of scope, . . . of taking on the provision of additional products at low incremental costs. . . . [A mandated] structural separation of services using common facilities would interfere with or totally prevent the achievement [of these economies when they are present]. (42–43)

Transfers of Functions from Regulated to Unregulated Sectors

An issue remaining in abeyance in current utility regulation is the question as to *which* subfunctions of the integrated electric industry (remaining after the transfer of the main function of generation) should be divorced from the regulated sector. These include subfunctions such as metering, billing, and bill collection, and may also be expanded to include specific components of the generation function itself, such as distributed generation. If these activities are to be divorced, the issue of *how* must be faced.

Distinguishing between essential and nonessential services (essential services are illustrated as access to transmission and distribution lines), Kahn lays down his standard for the transfer of the latter: "Considerations of pure economic efficiency would require that transfers of other-than-essential services be at bare marginal or incremental costs" (47).

Kahn sees violations of this standard as opening-up "cross-subsidization," a term "whose strict economic meaning is the offer of a service at rates below incremental costs . . . with the resulting incremental revenue deficiency being made good by other . . . services" (49).

Letting Go: **Deregulating the Process of Deregulation, 1998**[10]

Excerpts from Kahn's latest work, *Letting Go*, are included because they are relevant to any changes in the antitrust laws that might be considered, particularly if these changes were designed to favor new ventures.[11]

Where the quotations refer to a utility or utilities, the reader is invited to substitute the software industry or any other like industry, where entrenched firms face competition from newcomers.

It is interesting to recall that Summers, quoted in chapter 2, mentions the "creative destruction" that results from competition. This is paralleled by Kahn. As Kahn is quoted under "New Services" below, he refers to Schumpeter's characterization of innovation as "a process of creative destruction."

Competition Better than Regulated Monopoly

> I yield to no one in the intensity of my conviction that competition is a
> better safeguard and promoter of the interest of both consumers and the

public at large than regulated monopoly, wherever it is feasible—that is, except in cases where monopoly is natural, because competitive duplication of facilities would be grossly inefficient. Indeed, newly liberated competition can, in some circumstances, produce large and quick net public benefits. (2)

Preferences

Regulators are subject to "the temptation to produce some competitors, even competitors less efficient than the incumbents, by extending to them special preferences or protections and restraining efficient competitive responses by the incumbents" (16). One such preference is favoritism to "infant companies." Restraints are often urged by would-be competitors on the basis that "utility companies enjoy various competitive advantages over them that must be either offset or denied them if competition is to thrive" (22).

Some threats to efficient competition are undeniable, such as interference with the fair access of competitors or cross-subsidization by utilities of competitive activities. But one alleged threat that "is clearly not justified is the contention that rivals of . . . electric utilities require some special protections or preferences merely because the incumbent companies are in a position *to exploit economies* that are not available to their challenger" (23).

Integration and Competition

1. Integration as a Competitive Phenomenon

. . . competitive advantages arising out of economies of scale and scope are precisely the kind of efficiency advantages that we expect and want to prevail under competition. Integration is fundamentally a competitive phenomenon, and such efficiency advantages as it confers on the integrated firms are socially beneficent. The first fundamental competitive principle of freedom of entry means, first and foremost under conditions of real-world competition, freedom of existing firms to integrate into other operations or markets that they think they have special qualifications to serve.

2. The Beneficence of Economics of Scale and Scope

Competition by integration of existing firms into related markets is most likely to be socially productive precisely because it represents an attempt to achieve the benefits of economies of scope, the manifestation of which is the ability of a firm to supply a number of products or services in combination at lower costs than if it were to supply them separately. The source of such economies is the possibility—indeed, the pervasive phenomenon—of existing firms having special capabilities (physical plant, managerial or labor forces, technological or marketing skills or reputations) of taking on the provision of additional products or services at low incremental costs. (23–24)

Sources of possible economies would be input sharing; knowledge economies; and marketing economies (including familiar brand names, an economy of scope, the benefits of which would be anticompetitive to deny) (25–28).

The economies of scale and scope are open to competitors as well as incumbents. Competitors see "the opportunity to take advantage of exactly the same kinds and sources of economies of scope . . ." (30–31).

The asymmetrical imposition on incumbent firms of the obligation to share with competitors at prescribed discounts all service and marketing offerings and innovations, both present and future, may or may not be justified by the logic of "infant company" considerations, as a transitional expedient. Clearly, however—just as categorical prohibitions on incumbent firms offering particular services or denying them the right to fully reflect economies of scope in their pricing of competitive services or requiring them to share with competitors any or all sources of such competitive advantages as they may develop in the future—it conflicts in fundamental ways with the dictates of competition. (51)

The result is a continuing tension between the regulatory interventions necessary to ensure entrants a fair opportunity to compete and an understandable inclination to go farther and protect challengers—at least on a transitional basis—from disadvantages stemming from superior efficiencies enjoyed by the incumbents because of their inherited monopolies, superior enterprise, innovation, or luck. (52–53)

New Services

The provision of new services, and whether they should be regulated or not if offered by a utility company, is a subject of dispute in California and elsewhere. Kahn's view is clear-cut:

Under a proper conception of effective competition, the general rule, I believe, is that new services should not be subject to regulation—or, in the present context, to any obligations that they be shared with competitors. As Professor Joseph A. Schumpeter eloquently contended years ago, the conception of monopoly in the offer of truly new services is a virtual oxymoron. New services offer customers additional alternatives not available to them previously. Their introduction is fundamentally a competitive rather than a monopolistic phenomenon, even though they may be distinctive and the innovator may be in position to earn supernormal profits from them. Innovation—which Schumpeter characterized graphically as a "process of creative destruction"—is a profoundly competitive phenomenon that both creates new, temporary monopolies and destroys pre-existing ones. Those temporary monopolies—such as are conferred, for example, by patents—provide both the necessary incentive and reward for risk-taking innovation, the primary key to economic progress. To deny an innovator the rewards of being first would inhibit innovation, and it should not matter for these purposes whether the innovator is an incumbent . . . company or a new entrant. (59)

Prices and Cost (the Doctrine in Unregulated Markets)

In unregulated markets, prices tend to be set on the basis of the actual costs of incumbent firms, and they should be. The economic purpose of prices set at incremental cost is to inform buyers—and make them pay—the cost that society will actually incur if they purchase more or would actually save if they reduced their purchases, entirely or partially. These can only be the costs of the supplier whose prices are being set, not some hypothetical ideal producer. Moreover, such prices give challengers the proper target at which to shoot—the proper standard to meet or beat and the proper reward if they succeed. If they can achieve costs lower than that, they will enter and in the process . . . beat prices down to efficient levels.

In contrast [if rates should be set lower than actual costs due to the peculiarities of an allocation process, this] would actually discourage competitors coming in and building their own facilities. . . . (96)

Under the heading "The Competitive Benchmark," Kahn has this to say (quoting only in part):

Suppose society chose to subsidize a particular service that it hoped would be supplied competitively if the combination of regulated price and subsidy were right. The first measure required would be the amount by which the price necessary to elicit the desired supply in an unsubsidized market exceeded the price society was prepared to see charged consumers directly. That price would have to cover incremental costs. In addition, it would, in the presence of large economies of scale and scope, have to incorporate markups contributing to the recovery of total economic—i.e., current and forward-looking—costs. Moreover, as I have already expounded the case, it would incorporate an additional markup for the recovery of sunk costs of the incumbent supplier. As is also widely understood, finally, if those various markups were to be efficient—i.e., were to minimize the inefficiencies consequent on the necessity to set prices above marginal cost—they would as a general proposition vary inversely with the elasticities of the demands for the several services. (122)

Joint and Common Costs (and Opportunity Costs)

Letting Go states the usual distinction between joint and common products and their costs, plus a clarification on opportunity costs.

> The critical distinction [between joint and common products] is that joint products—strictly defined as products economically producible only in fixed, invariable proportions—do not have separate marginal production costs, whereas products produced in common do have such costs, which can be ascertained by increasing or decreasing the output of one of them while holding the others constant. (77)
>
> . . .
>
> . . . while joint products do not have separate marginal production or supply costs, they nevertheless have differing marginal opportunity costs and, correspondingly, efficient prices. A natural gas pipeline, similarly, provides capacity to carry gas "jointly" in summer and winter, a carpentry shop "jointly" to produce lumber and sawdust. The relevant economic question is what is added to society's costs if consumers purchase somewhat more, and what costs would society save if they purchased somewhat less, of the products for which that capacity is an input. (77–78)

Pricing Discrimination in Complementary Services

Kahn observes "a great deal of price discrimination in favor of demand-elastic or low 'value-of-service' customers" (80). Among the examples of this would be give-away credit card service with high interest charges, the "big money" being in the interest. He concludes that "where prices uniformly set at marginal costs would not recover total costs, such price discrimination can clearly be welfare-enhancing. . . . However, this justification does not apply to or justify the underpricing of services . . . having incremental costs which are very high and the demand highly inelastic relative to those of [the other service]" (81).

5. School Vouchers
An Illustration of the Methodology

The question of whether or not school vouchers should be issued is highly controversial, and promises to remain so. Emotions run high. The national parties are split—one in favor, the other opposed. Public opinion mirrors the same division. This chapter takes no position on either side. Its purpose is to clarify, not to decide.

Data on impacts of a voucher program, as cited by advocates and opponents (and within each group), are wildly at variance. Divergent statistics do not serve the public interest. A degree of certainty should replace vague claims and counterclaims. Only in this fashion will voters have a solid factual basis for their choice. This suggests uniformity in the calculation of impacts, rather than hit-or-miss speculations advanced to support one view or the other.

This chapter proposes that marginal cost methodology be adopted to gain the desired uniformity. This methodology stems from the normative microeconomic proposition that marginal cost determinations move the economy in the right direction. If this is the right direction for the economy

Acknowledgments: I appreciate the cooperation of the Portland Public Schools (School District No. 1, Multnomah County, Oregon) in making available its budget for 2000–2001, a thorough and well-prepared document. Special thanks are expressed to Lynn Ward, budget officer, for her valuable help in interpreting the document. The base data for this study are derived from the district's 2000–2001 budget, but the district has no responsibility for my methodology or any of my adjustments or conclusions.

as a whole, it should be the right direction for what is perhaps the single most important sector of the economy, the education of our children. In this sector, school vouchers may be the most highly contested issue.

School Vouchers Defined

For present purposes, a school voucher is defined in general terms as a payment to parents who choose to move their child from a public school to a different mode of instruction (which might be a private school, a charter school, a public school in a different school district, or tutoring, as the parents might select). The purpose of the payment is to partially reimburse parents for the additional cost of the alternative instruction.

Basic Assumptions

Comporting with the fundamental premise of microeconomics that resources are limited, it is assumed that education funds overall are limited. From this basic premise the rigorous follow-up assumption is adopted that expenditures for voucher payments will result in a commensurate reduction in the funding available to the affected public school for its continuing operations. It is further assumed that this reduction in funding for the affected public school will occur regardless of the source of its funds, whether that source is local, state, or federal (Title 1 or other federal source).

Objectives

The illustrative analysis that follows seeks to approximate two figures: (1) the maximum amount of the voucher allowance that might reasonably be provided, and (2) the voucher's effect upon the funding that remains available to the affected public school district for its reduced student body.

Time Frames

Short-Run Marginal Cost and Intermediate-Run Marginal Cost

These approximations are made for two alternative time frames, both representative of the marginal cost approach. First is the short-run marginal cost (SRMC), which measures the costs incurred, or avoided, as the near-immediate result of the program change. For the purposes of this analysis, it is the *avoided* cost to the public school that is relevant (as distinct from the cost *incurred* by the substituted mode of instruction). The program change is the transfer of students from the public school.

The short-run analysis includes only the incremental (i.e., the marginal) changes in costs that would be experienced in the near future in the expenditures of the school from which the students are transferred. In all likelihood, only direct instruction costs would vary in this short period. "Sticky" variable costs would not be expected to respond as quickly, most probably remaining unchanged. Overheads, being relatively fixed, would remain constant.

Involving a somewhat longer period, the intermediate-run marginal cost (IRMC), would measure not only the immediately variable instruction costs but also other changes in variably sticky costs that could be made with time and opportunity for these adjustments. Again, little change in overhead costs would be expected.

Long-Run Marginal Cost

Although long-run marginal costs (LRMC) can be approximated with a degree of confidence for a corporate activity, it seems inappropriate to attempt to do so for a public school system. The imponderables are too many. A fully developed long-run view of a school system would necessitate: (a) *for present programs*, the substitution of new state-of-the-art programs adapted to future conditions—what would these new programs be? (b) *for the present organization*, the substitution of a revamped and streamlined organizational structure—along what lines would this structure be developed? and (c) *for the present mix of old and recent plant*, the substitution of modern, highly efficient facilities—a result virtually impossible to bring about for a school district even in theory. Any shortcuts in the above conditions (a modified LRMC) would be almost as speculative. It is concluded that, while LRMC might be an intriguing academic study, it is ill suited for present purposes, which aim at eliminating confusion, not compounding it.

In any event, there is a big difference between a corporate entity and a public education system that precludes serious consideration of LRMC for the latter. The school system, unlike the factory, must always be in place and always operational. Both SRMC and IRMC are consistent with this requirement for continuity of operations: LRMC is not.

The Marginal Unit of Measurement

Marginal theory suggests that the measurement unit should be as small as practicable. In the present case, the smallest possible unit would be a single student—obviously too small, for a teaching staff is not increased or decreased by reason of one student more or one less. So, how many students to be added, or in this case to be lost, should comprise the marginal unit?

Because the major variable cost in this study is the cost of instruction, it seems logical to adopt the number of students instructed *per teacher* as the marginal unit. With the present student-to-teacher ratio of 12 : 6 for the school district studied, the unit would comprise 12.6 students. In other words, 12.6 additional students would necessitate one additional teacher, or the loss of 12.6 students under a voucher program would avoid the cost of one teacher.

The illustrative school district serves 53,746 students. Assumptions regarding the number of students who might transfer under a voucher program must be fairly large, but on the other hand should not be excessive. Arbitrarily, for the short run, the transfer of about 1,008 students, or 80 marginal units, representing avoided costs for 80 teachers is assumed. For the intermediate run, these figures are increased by 50 percent, to 1,512 students, 120 marginal units, avoiding costs for 120 teachers. These two conditions reduce the student body by slightly less than 2 percent and 3 percent, respectively.

These inputs for the two time frames of the study are tabulated below:

	Short run	Intermediate run
Transfer students	1,008	1,512
Avoided teachers	80	120

The Base Budget

As a sample on which to base the calculations of this study, the actual budget for the school year 2000/2001 of a public school system of intermediate size is adopted. This system serves an area of 152 square miles, in which are 63 elementary, 17 middle, 10 secondary, and 10 special schools. It has 6,600 employees. Its enrollment for 2000/2001 is 53,746 students and its annual expenditures total $583.2 million, of which federal sources provide $44 million (7.5 percent). Expenditures per student average $10,851 per year.

Table 5.1 gives a breakdown of total expenditures by function. The data shown are the basis for the calculations that follow. Table 5.1 is not intended to be either typical or representative of school districts throughout the United States. It is a sample only. The calculations, therefore, present only sample results.

Line 18 shows that total variable costs of $412.8 million comprise 70.8 percent of the total annual budget. These are the costs that can be expected to change with changes in the number of students. Total fixed costs, which are likely to remain constant even in the face of modest variations in the student population, are given on line 32. These fixed costs total $168.2 million, 28.8 percent of the total budget. The balance of the total budget is an allowance for contingencies of $2.2 million, 0.4 percent.

Table 5.1 also shows personnel requirements, stated as "full-time equivalent positions" or "fte."

The Student-Teacher Ratio

The adopted student-teacher ratio, cited earlier is calculated below:

	Full-time equivalents
Instructors	
Instruction (Table 5.1, Line 8)	3,951.74
Instructional support: Students and staff	
(Table 5.1, Line 10, 11)	311.39
Total instructors	4,263.13
Ratio, students to instructors, 53,746 to 4,263.13, rounds to 12.6 : 1	

The Short Run

As mentioned earlier, a transfer of 1,008 students is taken as illustrative for the short run. This would avoid the need for 80 instructors.

Expenditures for salary and benefits are as follows:

	Full-time equivalents	Expenditures
Instruction	3,951.74	$271,621,053
Instructional support		
Students	122.15	9,297,048
Instructional staff	189.24	33,465,293
Total	4,263.13	$314,383,394
The average expenditure per instructor is $73,745.00		

Table 5.1

Base Budget

	Required personnel—FTE	Dollar amount	Percent of total
1. Instruction			
2. Early childhood education	96.13	5,812,621	
3. Elementary school	1,474.21	97,513,905	
4. Middle school	569.43	37,372,104	
5. Secondary school	706.54	58,997,710	
6. Special education	910.43	53,576,989	
7. Other services	195.00	18,347,724	
8. Subtotal	3,951.74	271,621,053	46.6
9. Instruction support			
10. Students	122.15	9,297,048	
11. Instructional staff	189.24	33,465,293	
12. School administration	319.98	29,946,171	
13. Student transportation	15.00	14,421,863	
14. Subtotal	646.37	87,130,375	14.9
15. Other support—variable			
16. Cafeteria and food service	296.50	15,757,882	2.7
17. Operation/maintenance of plant	516.48	38,249,394	6.6
18. Subtotal—variable costs	5,411.09	412,758,704	70.8
19. Other Support—fixed costs			
20. Administrative overhead			
21. Administration	46.24	6,196,741	
22. Business	90.50	7,734,148	
23. Central	100.85	9,803,885	
24. Subtotal	237.59	23,734,774	4.0
25. Community services	15.50	926,957	0.2
26. Financial requirements			
27. Capital improvements		96,591,974	16.6
28. Debt service			
29. Repayment of principal		35,250,000	6.0
30. Interest		11,702,559	2.0
31. Subtotal		46,952,559	8.0
32. Subtotal—fixed costs	253.09	168,206,264	28.8
33. Contingency fund		2,221,804	0.4
34. Total budget	5,664.18	583,186,772	100.0

Because the employment of 80 instructors is avoided by this transfer of 1,008 students, the avoided costs amount to $5,899,600. For the short run, this amount is considered to be the total avoided costs. Other associated costs vary with the number of students, but reduction in these other costs may not be achievable in the short run because of lags or similar stickiness.

These results suggest that a voucher in favor of each of the 1,008 transferring students could be issued in an amount up to $5,853 without detriment to the financial viability of the school district. If the voucher amount was less, the district would gain. Furthermore, the district would gain to the extent that noninstruction variable costs also could be reduced, but consideration of these other variable costs is deferred until the intermediate run is considered.

The Intermediate Run

For this time frame, the starting point is moved farther into the future, giving sufficient time to accomplish cost cutbacks in some of the sticky variable costs.

This somewhat extended time perspective assumes that the number of transferring students will increase from 1,008 to 1,512, making possible an increase in the reduction in direct instructional personnel from 80 to 120 at the same student-teacher ratio of 12.6 : 1. A reduction in the teaching staff of this magnitude produces savings in salaries and benefits of $8,849,400.

Other costs that may vary with the size of the student body are:

	Expenditures
School administration (Table 5.1, Line 12)	$29,946,171
Student transportation (Table 5.1, Line 13)	14,421,863
Cafeteria and food service (Table 5.1, Line 16)	15,757,882
Operation and maintenance of plant (Table 5.1, Line 17)	38,249,394
	$98,375,310

The above elements of costs present the always controversial problem of allocation: To what extent are costs reduced by a smaller student body? Undoubtedly, many sophisticated theories could be advanced for the allocation of each of these elements, but for purposes of this illustrative allocation, the following simplistic relationship is adopted as a basis for three of the four variable cost elements.

Number of transferring students	=	1,512	=	2.81 percent
Total number of students per budget		53,746		

It seems reasonable that cafeteria and food service costs would be reduced by this full percentage, 2.81 percent. Plant to be operated and maintained should be less after the loss of 1,512 students, but probably not to the same full extent. Arbitrarily, as illustrative, a drop of 2 percent in this expenditure element is assumed. School administration, the most sticky, may be more difficult to reduce. Arbitrarily, a saving of only 1 percent is assumed. Data are available that permit the substitution of a somewhat more refined procedure for the allocation of the student transportation function, $14,421,863. Only 11,231 students are transported by the district, about 23 percent of average daily enrollment. The cost per student transported averages $1,284. Assuming that a downward adjusted percentage of the 1,512 transfer students would use district facilities, 248 fewer students would be transported. At the average cost of $1,284 per student, this would result in a cost saving of $318,432.

The assumed avoided costs for these variable elements are:

	Percent	Avoided expenditures
School administration	1.00	$ 299,462
Student transportation	—	318,432
Cafeteria and food service	2.81	442,796
Operation and maintenance of plant	2.00	764,988
Total		$1,825,678

The above allocations of joint variable costs bring total avoided costs in the intermediate run to $10,675,078, or $7,060 per transferred student. If voucher payments per student do not exceed this amount, there would be no detrimental result to the school district.

In the intermediate run, overhead administrative costs are not reduced to accompany the reduction in students. They are viewed as common fixed costs, although arguably they might, in part at least, be considered variable. These costs are as follows:

	Full-time equivalents	Overhead expenditures
Administration	46.24	$ 6,196,741
Business	90.50	7,734,148
Central	100.85	9,803,885
Total	237.59	$23,734,774

The base budget also includes $926,957 for community services and $2,221,804 for contingencies as well as capital costs of $143,544,533.

School voucher conclusions are recapitulated below:

	Short run	Intermediate run
Number of transferred students	1,008	1,512
Avoided costs (dollars)		
Instruction	5,899,600	8,849,400
Other variables	—	1,825,678
Total	5,899,600	10,675,078
Avoided cost per student	5,853	7,060

Table 5.2 compares the base budget as shown in Table 5.1 with the new budget, as adjusted to reflect intermediate-run reductions because of the assumed student transfers. Table 5.2 rearranges some functions and adds subtotals.

Both the base budget and the revised intermediate-run budget reflect the same total dollar requirements. The revised budget shows the subtraction of avoided costs from the affected functions, which is compensated for by the addition of a new voucher fund from which voucher payments could be drawn. The fund covers the total amount that would be required to provide voucher payments for each of the 1,512 students assumed to be transferred, in the amount of $7,060 each, the full amount of the avoided costs (with a slight surplus in the fund due to rounding). If the voucher allowance was set at less than $7,060 per student, or if fewer students were transferred, the fund could be established with a lower total. If the allowance was more, or if a greater number of students transferred, the fund might have to be increased, depending upon the net effect, with a commensurate increase in the district's total requirements.

Tentative Results, with Cautions

Assuming the dollar amounts calculated above fall within a range of reasonableness, the study finds that the savings resulting from a modest transfer of students to a voucher program (1,512 students from a starting student body of 53,746), could be financed by a voucher allowance of up to $7,060 per transferring student, without detriment to the financing by the school district of its remaining obligations. If the voucher allowance falls short of $7,060, the shortfall benefits the

Table 5.2

Base Budget Compared to Adjusted Intermediate-Run Budget

Function	Base budget		Adjustments ($)	Adjusted budget	
	Expenditures ($)	Percent of total		Expenditures ($)	Percent of total
Instruction	271,621,053				
Instruction support					
Students	9,297,048				
Instructional staff	33,465,293				
Subtotal	314,383,394	53.9	(8,849,400)	305,533,994	52.4
School administration	29,946,171	5.1	(299,462)	29,646,709	5.1
Student transportation	14,421,863	2.5	(318,432)	14,103,431	2.4
Other support-variables					
Cafeteria and food service	15,757,882	2.7	(442,796)	15,315,086	2.6
Operation/maintenance of plant	38,249,394	6.6	(764,988)	37,484,406	6.4
Subtotal: variable costs	412,758,704	70.8	(10,675,078)	402,083,626	68.9
Other support-fixed costs					
Administrative overhead	23,734,774	4.0		23,734,774	4.0
Community services	926,957	0.2		926,957	0.2
Financial requirements	143,544,533	24.6		143,544,533	24.6
Subtotal: fixed costs	168,206,264	28.8		168,206,264	28.8
Contingency fund	2,221,804	0.4		2,221,804	0.4
Voucher fund				10,675,078	1.9
Total	583,186,772	100.0		583,186,772	100.0

district; if it exceeds $7,060, the district loses the excess and would be disadvantaged.

Even if these conclusions could be accepted as typical (and it would be sheer happenstance if they were typical), the study as outlined suffers from oversimplifications in a number of respects.

First, the study is essentially static in its perspective, like a snapshot picturing a given moment in time, with movement frozen. This is a *ceteris paribus* perspective. Marginal cost analysis is not that abstract. It should be dynamic, not static. It should address *movement at the margin* whenever it is possible to take movement into account.

An example is the adoption of a *static* student-teacher ratio. This budgeted figure disregards the tendency toward a declining ratio, which would take account of pressures to reduce classroom sizes (or their reverse, if that was anticipated). A dynamic ratio, measuring conditions *at the margin*, would be better. The ratio also suffers because it is predicated on *average* not *marginal* conditions. An undue reliance on averaged data should be avoided in a marginal cost study. However, these objections to the ratio are largely theoretical, and could not be avoided in the instant case.

A second oversimplification is the assumption that total funding for the district will not be reduced with a decline in students, beyond the net of expenditures the district is able to avoid because of the student transfer, less an allowance for voucher outlays. But it is possible that total funding available to a given district might be reduced by more than the net of savings less voucher expense, in which event the district would experience a budget deficit. This could occur—although ideally it should not occur—because of aberrations (such as using weighted student totals) in the formulas followed by the state in distributing state education funds among districts. Charter schools within a district might be exempt from causing this possibility.

Essentially, the study assumes that public school education funding, from whatever combination of sources, will remain a constant in total except for changes resulting from a voucher program. These changes are (1) the *addition* of voucher allowances to the expenses to be funded, and (2) the *subtraction* of the savings in costs resulting from the student transfers. If the voucher cost is less than the savings, funding for the district is improved; if the voucher cost is more, such funding falls short. Logically, the former should be expected because the program shifts the entirety of the educational burden from the public to the private domain, except for the voucher allowances. Private sources pick up the substantial body of costs not covered by the allowances, reducing the public school burden by that amount. To illustrate, using the data of this study, average per student costs are $10,851. Assuming the voucher allowance to be set at the full amount of the avoided costs, $7,060, the alternative mode of instruction would be required to provide $3,791 per student of private funds.

A third oversimplification is consideration of the school district as a whole, without distinguishing its components. Costs of these components differ widely. The components, shown in Table 5.1, extend from early childhood education, through elementary, middle, and secondary schools, to special education. To be more accurate, there should be a different voucher allowance, derived from appropriate avoided costs, for each type of education. The amount of the voucher allowance for the transfer of a high school student should not be the same as for the transfer of an elementary school student. This is an important caution with regard to the study's averaged voucher allowance and its associated averaged cost savings.

A fourth oversimplification is acceptance in the study of the broad functional classifications shown in the budget without examination of the individual cost elements included in the function. Thus "overhead" is considered to be a fixed cost that does not vary as the number of students declines. Overhead comprises administration, business, and central support services. While a superintendent is needed in any event, other cost elements might be variable. This particular oversimplification is explained by noting that the transfer of students assumed in the study is minor. If transfers were drastic in number, it is probable that overhead costs would be appreciably reduced.

A final oversimplification is that the study fails to recognize the assertion made by the district's administration, that additional services are needed, over and above those covered in the budget. The reason for this omission is simple. The data on these services are not given in the budget in a form that could be incorporated in this study. On this score it is also noted, rather ruefully, that no budget is ever considered by its authors to be ample. Always, there is more to be done.

Considering the foregoing cautions, it is emphasized that this chapter is not to be read as a finale to the "battle over numbers" on school vouchers. It is hoped that the figures presented will be sufficiently valid as to suggest a range of probable conclusions. That may or may not be the case. In any event the purpose of chapter 5 is different. Its objective is to suggest a *method of analysis* that could be followed as a *uniform approach* to school voucher issues, resulting in consistency in the values suggested by interested parties. That consistency, not any individual number, is the purpose of the study. Minimizing the obfuscations of the arguments caused by conflicting and confusing cost-benefit claims is its sole purpose.

6. Special Cases
Mixed Issues/Mixed Methodologies

Context and Background

Research Per Se

The base marginal cost methodology fits neatly into the analysis of a number of public policy issues, such as the school voucher issue illustrated in chapter 5. It is more complex to apply in the types of situations mentioned by Summers (chapter 1),[1] where minor marginal costs of increasing production are overwhelmed by the costs of recovering prior massive research and development (R&D)[2] investments. Research may be the largest single component of total costs. Prescription drugs and computer software seem to be conspicuous examples of this "special case" relationship in the New Economy.

The cost of an additional batch of a prescription drug is accepted as being small for most drugs, involving only the costs of component chemicals for the batch and the costs of added factory time.[3] These costs will vary, of course, with individual drugs, probably being higher for a vaccine than for a pill. But overall, the marginal cost of production will be much less than the cost of the laborious and lengthy R&D process of discovering and perfecting the drug's formula, and testing its effectiveness. This process includes many failed attempts.

Computer software presents a similar picture. It is inexpensive to run off additional copies of a software program, but hugely expensive to derive the program in the first place. Many trial programs may be written but disregarded because of defects before the final version is firmed up.

In sum, research is risky. But risk is not unique to drugs and software, nor is risk unique to the New Economy. There are parallels in the Old Economy as well, one of which (petroleum exploration) is outlined in more detail at a later point in this chapter.

The conventional application of the marginal cost model measures the incremental change in costs because of a change in the volume of output. This change is straightforward when easily measurable units of output are involved, such as an expansion of the number of kilowatt-hours produced by an electricity generation plant, the number of tons of steel manufactured by a steel mill, or the number of bushels of wheat grown by a wheat farmer. These changes are important for the examples mentioned because the costs incurred are significant in magnitude and may directly influence the market price. For these two reasons, the conventional methodology remains applicable in a quantitative environment.

The Information Age, on the other hand, demands measurements that are more qualitative than quantitative. Although the principle of the methodology remains the same, its application must be tempered to reflect a less tangible, broader perspective. This new environment looks to innovation, new ideas, as the marginal change in output, in substitution for a change in the output of an already known product or service. The costs of recycling an existing drug or an existing software program, or any other known product unique to the Information Age, become almost irrelevant when the innovation objective is paramount.

The shift from evaluating costs of output changes for a known product to costs necessary to induce innovative new products increases exponentially the complexity of a marginal cost analysis. This is so because a shift in costs for a known product is relatively easy to determine. The cost inputs are tangible, at least relatively so. But a shift in costs for a new product entails a shift from physical productivity to idea productivity, a shift from the tangible to the intangible. The revised approach to the analysis requires that the costs of a new concept having social value be measured in terms of the costs of the research and development efforts necessary to bring it about. This seemingly simple statement of the end result sought by the study hides its near-imponderable details.

Research Questions

How much R&D is necessary to bring forth an innovation? This is the basic question. Its answer necessitates consideration of many other questions. The manufacture of drugs is taken as illustrative. Because R&D precedes the new drug, this year's R&D does not correlate with this year's drug output. There is a lag between the two, but how much of a lag? Research and development in pursuit of a given remedy may extend over several years. How many? Some R&D is unproductive, resulting in failure. How much failed effort? The success-to-failure rate of R&D is volatile, in some years good, in others bad. How are "normal" results to be gauged? Some manufacturers have better luck in their R&D than others. Can an analysis based upon the experience of a single manufacturer be valid, or must the analysis be expanded to include manufacturers as a group? Research and development efforts may be concentrated on different objectives: entirely new products; improvement of existing products; or development of generic products to replace existing products. Should these groupings be composited in the analysis, or handled separately?

Some activities are related to, but outside of, the research umbrella. Sales expenses as generally defined are a major example. Each new drug has its own particular benefits, side effects, and instructions for use. Pharmaceutical companies employ trained representatives to advise hospitals, doctors, and pharmacists on proper usage. While these contacts are promotional as well as advisory, is the advising activity a necessary element in the development of the drug, and hence to be included in R&D costs? The same question applies to advertising, which often is informational as well as promotional. By what methods should sales expenses be apportioned between advisory, to be included in R&D costs, and promotion, to be excluded?

These are a sampling of the questions on R&D that the analyst must take into account when framing a drug study. A software inquiry would have to confront the same range of questions.

While questions such as these arise to some limited extent in almost every cost study, for drugs and software they are not peripheral but fundamental, looming much larger in reaching a valid end result. Peripheral factors can often be brushed aside in the usual study by adopting broad assumptions in lieu of specifics. This is not so here. That is why an R&D study points to additional refinements.

Some Clarifications

Expenditures for R&D are investment costs because they are made for the purpose of enabling later production. They serve the same function as dollars advanced for the construction of a new factory in which manufacturing activities will subsequently be conducted. In the New Economy R&D is singled out for special consideration, recognizing that it is only one type of investment, for two interrelated reasons: first, because innovation rests upon expensive research, and second, because innovative research is risky and involves highly uncertain results. The combination of high costs and speculative outcomes separates R&D investments from the investment mainstream. The closest parallel for this combination is the exploration function of oil and natural gas producers.

It is emphasized that Information Age R&D investments are not unique because of their size. High investment costs are also characteristic of most capital-intensive industries, such as the utilities. But the outcomes differ. For example, the huge investments necessary for an electricity generating plant are made with the certainty that the plant, when built, will be capable of generating electric power. There is little if any doubt that the dollars spent will result in a functioning facility. Neither the plant's operational capability nor the dollars invested in it are speculative. (There may be some doubt on the demand side, but that is a different matter.) In contrast, R&D expenditures for drugs and software may fail to produce any of the hoped-for results.

The Summers Focus: High Fixed, Low Variable Costs

It is also pointed out that the coupling of high investment costs with low production costs is not a unique combination. Citing the prior example, the actual costs of production of electricity per unit of output are small in comparison with per-unit capital costs. The same is true of many capital-intensive industries (although probably not to the same degree as for drugs and computer software).

This coupling presents no particular problem for economists—it has been observed and studied for years. The problem arises when a product having this cost characteristic emerges into the public eye *in a bad light*. It is difficult for the public to understand why a product that they need— such as a prescription drug—should be sold at an expensive price when it can be manufactured cheaply.

The foregoing discussion is limited to high R&D investment costs, rather than to high investment costs in general, so as to concentrate on speculative-type investments. High investment costs and low production costs are coupled because this linkage aggravates public resentment against market prices that are perceived to be excessive. Finally, research is deemed to be a "special case" because the analysis of speculative investment costs requires an elaborate extension of the marginal costing techniques outlined in chapter 3.

The Parallels

The Operational Parallel

In terms of risk, the exploratory function of the petroleum industry is a counterpart of the research function of pharmaceutical and software firms. Oil companies must search for and locate new oil and natural gas reserves in order to maintain production as old reserves are depleted, in the same fashion as Information Age industries must conduct research to discover new products.

The oil and gas search will begin with an examination of prospective drilling locations using surface technology, both geological and geophysical, including seismic surveys. Data are built up over the years, with each new search adding a bit of information. These examinations will point to locations that are considered promising, as well as to other locations that fall short. Some locations will be "rank wildcat," which are distant from producing areas or there is little prior information about them. Others will be closer to known fields already in production. (Parallel: review of prior data.)

Having determined a likely site, the producer must obtain a lease permitting drilling from the owner. For larger or better sites, many of which may be on government-controlled land or water, leases can be acquired only by competitive bidding at auction. Bids for the same site often cover a wide range—a $1 million bid by one company, a $10 million bid by another—showing extreme variations in the opinions of the individual bidders regarding the potential of the site and the cost of drilling. Awarded bid amounts are nonrefundable. Bidding is an initial, highly risky step. (Parallel: selecting the research objectives.)

Having secured a site, an exploratory well or wells must be drilled. The well may turn out to be a dry hole, or it may yield oil or natural gas.

No one knows. Drilling is a second highly risky step. (I have participated as an observer in a number of internal company debates that reveal the tensions of drilling decisions.) Something like the following may occur.

The company's geologists and geophysicists recommend drilling at a specific point on the acquired lease. They specify the maximum depth of the proposed exploratory well and its costs, together with its potential for production if successful. Per foot costs of drilling increase with depth. To illustrate, say that management approves drilling up to 15,000 feet at a cost of $7 million. The day arrives when the well has been drilled down to this depth, and $10 million has been spent. But so far, the well is a dry hole.

However, the company's experts still feel confident that reserves will be found if drilling is continued to a deeper depth. They recommend continuing for another thousand feet, with an additional cost of a few million dollars.

The question then is whether to walk off, having lost the entirety of the bid cost and the cost of the well to date, or to continue drilling, possibly throwing more good money after bad. There is little time for deliberation, for each hour of delay gives rise to the additional expense of holding the drilling rig at the site. This example is real. (Parallel: continuing or terminating research toward the selected objective when results to date have failed.)

It is pure hyperbole to comment that the entire process of exploration for oil and natural gas, including facing questions such as the above, is highly risky. The research function of pharmaceutical and software companies is analogous.

These parallels between petroleum exploration and Information Age research are not the whole of the comparability of the two otherwise different types of activities. For both, successful efforts are likely to be outnumbered by failures. Even successful efforts produce mixed results. For oil and gas, these range from the marginal well or field to the huge find, such as Prudhoe Bay; for drugs, they may lead to either a minor product improvement or an extremely popular new remedy such as Viagara; for software, the result may be only a minor shortcut to the Internet via a browser or a massive Windows.

Petroleum end products resulting from exploration differ in both quality and quantity. The producer may find oil only, or mixed oil and gas, or gas only. For oil, the product may be sour or sweet, light or heavy; for gas, the BTU content, the water content, or sulfur content, may vary. Other differences in product quality are many, and most of them affect the value of the product. Quantity is also a variable. One field may contain large reserves, another only minimal reserves. Drugs and software discovered by research also vary in quality, but future production volumes are not a factor because the firm can manufacture any desired quantity. Quantity of future output is a point of noncomparability.

Structurally the two groups are similar. Multiple producers are engaged in exploration for new reserves; numerous pharmaceutical and software companies are engaged in research for new products.

A further area of *probable* similarity relates to success-failure experience. The oil and gas success rate for any given producer will vary from year to year (not necessarily in ratio to its exploratory budget). Also, in any given year, the success rate for one producer may differ materially from that of other producers. Unfortunately, data for drugs and software are not available to permit a firm conclusion about whether drug and software success patterns also vary from year to year for the same firm, or in any given year from firm to firm. It is inferred that these variations occur because of the inherent uncertainty of research.

The above "probable" similarity is of major importance to any marginal cost study of drugs and software, particularly one aimed at a regulated price because, if the similarity holds, it rules out the adoption of a selected "test year" for the individual firm being studied, as has been the historical practice under utility regulatory procedures. Further, to arrive at representative results, the composite experience of a group of comparable firms over a span of years might have to be substituted for the "single firm" traditional pattern. This is a lesson learned from the natural gas regulatory experience.

There is an even more important lesson to be learned from prior experience, which is the reason that the similarities between petroleum exploration and Information Age research have been treated in detail. Simply put, the lesson is that speculative investments in research cannot be evaluated as simply as the nonspeculative investments in physical plant to which most regulatory attention has been devoted in the past. Evaluation of speculative research necessitates more complex procedures. The best clue is the nation's earlier experience in attempting price regulation for natural gas, which is recounted next.

Commentary on "The Operational Parallel" is closed with this caveat. These remarks do not purport to present an in-depth analysis of either the petroleum industry or the new Information Age industries. The above comparison is general in nature, having as its purpose only to draw the parallel between petroleum exploration (where natural gas price control was in place for a time) and the pharmaceutical industries (where price control is threatened).

The Regulatory Parallel

In 1954, prices of natural gas at the wellhead, the point of physical production, were brought under government control by a U.S. Supreme Court interpretation of the Natural Gas Act. This control was exercised by the then–Federal Power Commission (FPC), now the Federal Energy Regulatory Commission (FERC). The FPC had long controlled the prices of natural gas pipelines operating in interstate commerce, following traditional utility regulatory patterns.

Essentially, the traditional pattern involved determining a "cost of service" upon which the regulated price(s) would be based for the individual company whose operations were being reviewed. The FPC first tried to adopt this pattern for natural gas producer prices. The effort failed because the experience of a single producer whose operations were widespread could not be considered representative either of producer costs in general or of costs prevailing in any particular area. If followed, the result would be one price for gas produced by one producer while the price for gas produced by another producer, perhaps from an adjacent well, would be different, although the gas itself would be identical. It was soon recognized that price differences from well to well in the same locality that were caused by differences in the separately determined companywide costs of service for individual producers would reduce the market to chaos.

The FPC then abandoned its focus upon individual companies in favor of the group experience of producers within a broad producing area. This new focus was predicated upon the concepts (1) that group experience would be representative, and (2) that different prices from one broad geographical area to another would be workable. The result was a series of "area rate cases," of which the Permian Basin was the first.

To implement this effort, producers in the specified area were instructed to collaborate in the preparation and presentation of an area-wide cost of service. This was time consuming and very expensive for the affected producers as well as for the FPC. The turmoil of these cases is bypassed as being unnecessary for the present discussion. Finally, separate prices for "old" and "new" gas evolved, leading to what many considered to be irrational pricing. Old gas is neither more nor less valuable on the market than new gas. Both are the same to the consumer.

The eventual result was the abandonment of price control over natural gas wellhead prices. Presently, these prices are deregulated in favor of the free market.

It is pertinent to point out two central problems that confronted regulators in their attempts to regulate natural gas prices. The first was the necessity to allocate costs between two products that were produced in conjunction with each other, oil and natural gas. Thus, at the very outset of the regulatory process, an allocated wellhead cost of natural gas had to be determined. The second issue was how to determine an appropriate rate of return on investments that were highly risky. The return issue would be a central problem if attempts were made to institute price controls over drugs, software, and like endeavors.

Patents: The Missing Parallel

A huge difference between Old Economy exploration and New Economy research is that drugs (and, perhaps to a lesser extent, software) may be protected by patents that grant to the patentee a temporary monopoly, including freedom to price its product as it sees fit without direct competition during the patent period. Patent protection clearly reduces the research investment risk that the manufacturer otherwise would face. How would this reduced risk be evaluated in relation to the risk of research investments unprotected by patents?

Any imposition of price controls over patented products would introduce the necessity for a drastic change in existing patent law. However, it is possible under present law that cost/price considerations might enter into determinations on whether or not to extend existing patents. That would inject into the patent extension process the quasi-regulatory issue of future prices in relation to the recovery of past research investments as well as the coverage of current costs.

Either of these—a change in patent law or an enlargement of the horizon for patent extensions—appears to be a possibility that may emerge as a public policy issue as consumers grow impatient with present prices.

Lessons from the Parallels

For the New Economy, perhaps the most compelling economic lesson from the parallels is that price control, after being attempted over many years, was ultimately abandoned as unworkable and adverse to the public interest for a business activity having many of the characteristics of Information Age enterprises. Other lessons point to the complexity and uncertainty of the techniques that would have to be adopted to administer price control. These would be cumbersome and time consuming, and could be expected to hinder the rapid innovation expected from the New Economy.

However, these are only one person's conclusions. Each reader will draw her or his own conclusions from these parallels. They have been addressed in some detail to permit such individual evaluations, whether by the policy maker, the microeconomist, or the concerned bystander. These are the judgments that count.

Following are more specific conclusions, again with deference to any contrary opinions of the reader.

Re: Price Control

1. It would be futile to attempt direct price control over any individual product or an individual manufacturer. The effort would be doomed to failure, and during its pursuit might seriously inhibit the research activities of the manufacturer, dimming prospects for innovative new products that are the promise of the Information Age.

2. However, if demanded by the public, a generalized review of the profit prospects of a manufacturer could be introduced as part of the patent extension process. Such a review, if introduced, should be voluntary on the part of the applicant, and the applicant's burden of proof would be less than in adversarial proceedings that characterize utility price regulation. This being said, it must be admitted that any cost/price showing presents a substantial obstacle, even if voluntary, and would tend to grow in complexity over time.

3. Any attempt to impose direct price controls over drug or software manufacturers as a group, as distinct from individually, likewise would be futile, and utterly inconsistent with the

economics of these industries. Over and above these inconsistencies, price controls are slow moving and ponderous, at odds with the fast pace necessary to continue the New Economy's momentum in inducing innovation.

Re: Antitrust

In chapter 7, the view is expressed that the ultimate objective of the antitrust statutes—though unspoken in the laws—is the attainment of the lowest practicable prices for consumers. For this reason, certain impediments to competition are deemed illegal. The precise issue of price as such may or may not be raised in antitrust proceedings. In the still pending Microsoft case, the company's price does not seem to have been considered, possibly because it was thought to be low rather than high. Nonetheless, in many instances, such as whether mergers should be allowed or prohibited, logic suggests that a key element should be the impact of the merger upon the consumer price. If the consumer price will be reduced, that is a good argument in favor of the merger; if it will be raised, it is an argument against.

Such price questions point directly to the use of the marginal cost methodology. A general outlook for prices before and after the merger can be approximated by adopting this approach. The mechanics are difficult, beyond doubt, even for a broad approximation, and perhaps sound conclusions can be drawn from other data, market power, and so on. But if price to the consumer is the ultimate question, perhaps it should be addressed directly.

Applying the Methodology

Although price control is not recommended for any of the industries prominent in the New Economy, this does not imply that consideration of a cost-price relationship might not be valuable in a number of other circumstances. In fact, where costs (or the cost-to-price link) under one scenario are being compared to a different scenario, the marginal cost methodology is straightforward and will produce consistent answers regarding the impact of the varying situations being compared. This consistency is particularly important for the analysis of public policy issues. In some cases, the methodology outlined in chapter 3 can be applied without substantial modification, as was done in the school voucher study of chapter 5. In other cases, such as those where research costs are a major component of the price, extensions of the procedure are indicated. In still other cases, such as might arise in one guise or another in antitrust proceedings, either the base or a modified procedure might be most appropriate.

Under this heading, modifications are described in the base procedure that responds to a number of different situations, ranging from the simple to the more complex. Most of the suggestions, especially those concerned with research or antitrust, plow new ground. These are advanced with a great deal of humility. Others undoubtedly will propose better and easier routes to the same ends.

The Base Pattern

Whatever the subject of the cost analysis, steps 1 through 7 outlined in chapter 3 should be followed, namely, defining the problem, choosing the time frame and unit of measurement, obtaining the cost data and classifying costs, making any indicated allocations, and finally isolating the specific costs for which changes due to output variations (or other variations in conditions) are to be compared.

Step 3, choosing the unit of measurement, requires further elaboration. Unlike a change in output for an existing product or service, whether that is an additional known pill or additional students to be instructed, the unit of measurement for research is likely to be unknown at the beginning of the study. It may turn out to be an entirely new prescription drug, a new generic drug, an improvement in an existing drug, new software offering an original application of computer technology, improved software that is more reliable than glitch-prone existing programs, some combination of these, or whatever. This simply is not known. Even distinctions between pure and applied research do not help much. At the beginning of the study, then, it may not be possible to define the unit of measurement with any precision. All that can be said at this early juncture may be that the unit will be some new innovation, emerging from the research effort, which has positive social value. This skeleton definition will be fleshed out as the study progresses.

Although it has been taken for granted that production costs per unit of output will be less than R&D costs per unit of output, this may not actually be the case for any individual drug (such as the flu vaccine) or individual software program. The generalized hypothesis must be tested.

Therefore, the marginal cost of production should be found. Fortunately, the familiar pattern can be followed in determining production costs.

The Addition of Investment Costs

Investment costs are considered to be fixed and therefore ignored in the conventional marginal cost study, except for the very long-run marginal cost (LRMC) analysis. No such disregard for investment costs is possible where research expenditures are a primary variable cost element even in the short run. This seeming anomaly results from the fact that research must be continuous if it is to be effective in producing a stream of innovations. In contrast, physical plant additions need not be made continuously to maintain production. Thus, for the base model, plant can realistically be regarded as static. Research, in contrast, must be ongoing and dynamic.

Converting Expenditures to Costs

Expenditures give rise to an investment base, but of themselves they do not constitute cost. The cost of the expenditure is comprised of the rate of return *on* the outstanding investment and the recapture *of* the investment over time by the investor. (In the utility terminology, a return *on* and *of* the investment.) The return *on* the investment should be sufficient to cover the company's costs of the bonds and preferred stock in its capital structure, plus a reasonable (normal) rate of return on its equity component. The company's recapture of its invested dollars will be accomplished through depreciation (usually over a period of years for physical plant facilities) or through depletion allowances (as for investments in wells where the reserve of oil or natural gas supplying the well is drained as the oil or natural gas is produced: a so-called unit of production method). For drugs or software, presumably an appropriate method would spread recapture of the investment over the anticipated market life of the product.

If prior experience is any guide, the determination of a proper rate of return *on* the investment for drugs, software or like products would be illusive and controversial; and the methods for return *of* the investment would be equally so. Nevertheless, if a cost were to be determined, that process would be unavoidable. That is one reason why it has been concluded earlier that a full cost-of-service determination for industries characterized by high research costs would be futile. (In fact, this conclusion can be expanded to add that price controls, requiring such complex determinations, are to be avoided for *any* industry unless that industry is a natural monopoly for which the free market cannot be accepted as resulting in a reasonable price to consumers.)

Research investments are only a part of the investment base of a company, as mentioned earlier. Other types of investments would also have to be included in any full cost-of-service determination. This merely adds emphasis to the fundamental conclusion just stated.

Repeated again here is the major economic characteristic of research: It is risky. Its results cannot be foreseen; failures are mixed with successes, yet the cost of failures as well as the cost of successes must be recovered in price; even successful efforts will fluctuate in degree, a few being wildly popular products, many only marginal; and expenditures over a single period (say the historic utility "test year") are unlikely to be representative.

Suggestion

In view of these characteristics, it is suggested that any conversion of expenditures to cost be avoided. In partial substitution, total research expenditures over a span of years could be averaged. These total expenditures would include outlays for "dry holes" as well as productive ideas. It is to be expected that expenditures will vary from year to year because research budgets are affected by many extraneous considerations. A five-year span is suggested as a minimum. The purpose is to give a bird's-eye view of research outlays.

The Addition of Revenues

Revenues associated with research investments are difficult to gauge. Reliance cannot be placed upon the revenue stream of the manufacturer because revenues result from old as well as new products. The revenue stream must be untangled if revenues offsetting costs are to be included in the study.

To untangle, new concepts brought to the market would have to be identified, and the revenue derived from them would have to be isolated from the revenues associated with other products. This is easy to say, but such new concepts, and their resulting revenues, undoubtedly would be difficult to isolate. (It is not known whether manufacturers seek such differentiations for their internal purposes. If they do, the job would be simplified.) Essentially the task of isolation would be judgmental (whoever does the job) and therefore subject to challenge. This would not be unusual for a regulatory-type analysis.

Earlier it was stated that the unit of measurement for research would be new innovations, new ideas having social value, rather than units of already known products or services. Progressing from the general to the specific, the question of which innovations have social value now must be confronted. In response, resort can be made to the usual refuge of the economist, the market. The value of a new concept can be gauged by the revenues the manufacturer receives as the product is marketed. Such revenues reflect the value of the product to society (indicating what the consumer is willing to pay).

It is important to understand what product revenues do *not* measure. Overall, market prices are set to recover all costs of the manufacturer, but any individual price is a function of demand, not cost. Revenues arising from market prices are therefore not a measure of product costs in a multiproduct firm. With specific regard to research costs, the cost component for research in any given price may be anything from zero up, and certainly this component can vary materially from one product to another, whether the product is new or old. Therefore, product revenues are not a measure of research costs.

Suggestion

For these reasons, it is suggested as one possible method that the *collective* revenues for all new products (not each new product individually) be used as a yardstick to compare research costs with results. This comparison cannot be made over the same time periods because of the lag between research and sales. This lag is probably not uniform, but an effort should be made to take it into account. For example, cumulative research expenditures over the 1992–96 period could be compared to cumulative revenues from new products over the years 1996–2000, a five-year span of experience for both, with a one-year overlap. This would enable a rough approximation of the portion of a research dollar required to induce a revenue dollar.

It has not been suggested that each research expenditure be earmarked initially in terms of its goal, such as a cure for arthritis in drug research, because the end result may be completely different, say a remedy for high blood pressure. Nor has it been suggested that unsuccessful research be classified as such at the time when it seems evident to be a failure (a dry hole in our exploration parallel, or a program with too many glitches in our software parallel), for the results ultimately may turn out to be valuable.

An approach that eschews an individual year in favor of multiple years has its forerunner in the petroleum exploration precedent.

Alternatives

The conclusion that price controls requiring complex costing procedures should be avoided does not necessarily foreclose application of the general theory of the methodology on a more limited basis. The two suggestions above are incorporated in the following.

1. Assuming that the objective was limited to a showing of research expenditures in relation to product results, cumulative research expenditures over a past period (perhaps ten years in this case) could be compared with a list of the new improved products that have resulted from the research. This would be the simplest showing, but it would add substance to the heretofore generalized claim that extensive research expenditures are required to discover innovative products (if that was the result). It would comport with marginal theory because the new products listed were those discovered at the margin.

2. If the objective was somewhat broader, expanded to include a showing of research expenditures in relation to both product and revenue results, cumulative research expenditures over a past period could be compared with cumulative revenues from new products over the same period. Using the same period would demonstrate the lag. Using different but overlapping periods as mentioned earlier would assume a lag, but not demonstrate it.

Of course, neither of the above would validate the price charged for new products because research expenditures do not measure the costs of research investments, and because costs of other activities and of the other types of investment are included to one extent or another in the price. The study would show only broad relationships, but these would be valuable in improving public understanding of the role of research. (One would hesitate to try to foresee the results of such a showing. They are unknown to the public, and possibly vague even to the manufacturer.)

Cases (1) and (2) above seem to be applicable to both drugs and software. Case (3), which follows, is aimed at drugs only.

3. Assuming that the objective is to compare prices for new drug products sold domestically with prices for these products sold outside the United States, again in relation to research, the same cumulative expenditures for research could be compared with two separate cumulative revenue streams from new products, one from domestic sales and the other from foreign sales. This would reveal the extent to which research expenditures were covered in each group of sales, and the disparity between the two coverages. (Here it is taken for granted that a disparity exists.)

The above three cases beg one serious question, namely, to what extent should a portion of sales expense (which includes the costs of consultations with doctors, pharmacists, hospitals, and advertising) be added as being advisory rather than promotional? In other words, are advising efforts necessary to launch a new product evolving from the research expenditure, in which case they might reasonably be included as part of the expenditures for R&D. The arguments in favor are strong, but it might be advisable to avoid the difficult allocation problem of separating sales expense into advisory and promotional classifications. Perhaps a simple showing of sales expense in total, without allocation, would suffice. This not insignificant issue is left to the analyst.

4. If the objective was to examine the possible price results of a merger or other action requiring FTC or Justice Department approval, or if price was an issue in an antitrust case, base marginal cost methodology would be ideally suited, because this methodology measures cost changes at the margin where differences are key.

One benefit of this methodology is that, done properly, it will reveal the costs associated with a future change in output by the firm as presently structured (e.g., without a merger) and the same future changes in output (with the merger in place). The comparison thus takes into account before and after the merger's allocative and productive efficiencies as these terms are used by Judge Robert Bork. More generally, the analysis takes these efficiencies into account with and without the variable being studied.[4] Bork's definitions are:

> Allocative efficiency . . . refers to the placement of resources in the economy, the question of whether resources are employed in tasks where consumers

value their output most. Productive efficiency refers to the effective use of resources by particular firms. The idea of effective use . . . encompasses much more than mere technical or plant-level efficiency.[5] (91)

Bork explains:

> These two types of efficiency make up the overall efficiency that determines the level of our society's wealth, or consumer welfare. The whole task of antitrust can be summed up as the effort to improve allocative efficiency without impairing productive efficiency so greatly as to produce either no gain or loss in consumer welfare. That task must be guided by basic economic analysis, otherwise the law acts blindly upon forces it does not understand and produces results it does not intend.[6]

The normal procedure outlined in chapter 3 could be followed with these changes:

(a) The statements relating to the disregard of fixed costs under "Objective" at the beginning of chapter 3 must be changed to comport with the different objective of an antitrust-type of study, which would include some fixed costs. This comment also applies to Step 1. Defining the Problem. The problem will be in a different guise than mentioned in Step 1, but it is important that the purpose be carefully specified.

(b) Step 7, Cost Selection, would be eliminated. All variable costs would be included in the analysis, without omissions. The purpose of this change is to eliminate any challenges to the omissions that might otherwise be made.

(c) Step 8, The Marginal Cost Calculations, would be modified to cover only the variable costs in total, omitting costs per unit of product as introducing an unnecessary complication where the overall operations of a multiproduct firm, not just an individual product, are being studied.

(d) A meaningful analysis suited to the evaluation of a proposed merger, or similar questions, is deficient if fixed costs are entirely excluded from consideration—the study would be fatally incomplete and inconclusive. Some fixed costs must be included. For noninvestment fixed costs, such as overheads, the answer is easy. Just include these administrative costs in the study as variable, which they are likely to be in any event.

Investment costs also should be included, but in a fashion that would not require the complex and controversial issue of a proper rate of return on the outstanding investment. A simple substitute for the cost of invested capital (computed on the basis of the rule of a return on and of capital) would be to add to the study a statement of the outstanding investment before and after the merger (if a merger was the issue) or with or without the variable being studied (if a different issue was the subject). This addition would fall short of indicating an appropriate level of revenues, as is the end result of utility price regulation because total costs are not calculated, but it would be a significant indicator of relative operational efficiencies with respect to capital requirements in comparative situations.

If the levels of outstanding investments were to be shown as just suggested, it would be helpful, and a bow to the Information Age, if these investments were broken down into research and nonresearch classifications, isolating investments having a high-risk element in the former. It would also be helpful to distinguish the current year from earlier years.

Assuming a merger to be the subject, a before-merger study would be required for each of the proposed parties, together with an after-merger study for combined operations.

The inclusion of outstanding prior year investments (sunk investments) as an aid to evaluation as suggested here is not to be confused with the inclusion of sunk costs per se. The objective of the present study is not to arrive at a cost that would govern price. Instead, the instant study is to provide a yardstick for determining the comparative impacts of a proposed action. For this comparison, changes in investment levels are just as important as changes in operational outlays.

(e) Because the marginalist looks to the future (as should any government adjudicator), the comparative studies should contemplate a future output or a future level of operations. A future perspective provides enlightenment about the gain (or loss, if that is the case) in allocative and productive efficiencies, such as cost savings and economies of scale. It also suggests the negative societal results, loss of jobs in the workforce, lesser competition in the market, greater market power for the enlarged firm, and so forth, although it would not be conclusive regarding these possible negatives.

5. If the objective was to determine whether a drug patent should be extended, the methodology could be adopted in two versions.

(a) One version would follow the usual procedure, outlined in chapter 3, which would measure the variable costs associated with a future production level. This would indicate the minimum price at which the drug could be sold without loss to the manufacturer. This cost/price level could be compared with the price that the manufacturer could be expected to charge if the patent were to be extended. The overage of the latter over the former would indicate the price surplus that the manufacturer would have available to meet its fixed costs (operational, plus recovery of prior investment costs, including its embedded costs of research).

A comparison of these same variable cost results could also be made on the assumption that the patent would not be extended, forcing the manufacturer to sell in competition with a generic drug or whatever other competition the market might provide. Here again, the price surplus would measure the extent to which the manufacturer would have funds to meet its fixed costs, this time in a competitive rather than a protected market.

While far from conclusive, the difference between these two price surpluses might provide a guide as to whether or not the patent should be extended, by revealing the extent to which sunk costs (including research costs) could be recovered under either option.

(b) But suppose the issue of continuity of future research is interjected into a patent extension debate, an issue that may be at the heart of the pros and cons rather than the more arcane question of the recovery of sunk costs (although both go hand in hand). From this perspective, an increment for future research, over and above the marginal cost of production, should be included in the cost.

As previously pointed out, an expenditure for research is not equivalent to the cost of research (unless the expenditure is fully recovered in the year of incurrence), and it is undesirable to introduce unrecovered investment costs into the suggested procedures because of the complexity of determining a proper rate of return *on* and recovery *of* the investment in any given period.

It is also possible to refrain from doing so now, because there is a workable alternative. If the simple assumption can be accepted that the expenditures for research by the manufacturer in the prior period (say the average over the prior five years) during which the patent was in force were representative of the research expenditures that the manufacturer would continue to make if the patent were to be extended, this average amount for research could be added to the variable costs found in the marginal cost study.

The purist in the regulatory tradition will point out that this result would undercut the manufacturer's actual costs by reason of the fact that the above marginal cost analysis (1) includes only variable costs, thus omitting fixed overhead costs, such as property taxes, which are real, (2) excludes income taxes, which are real, and (3) excludes recovery of sunk investment costs that is necessary for long-term viability. With respect to the first point, it would be reasonable to include an increment for overhead. The other points are different. This is not a price-fixing exercise looking toward a controlled price. Its purpose is to shed light upon whether or not a patent extension should be granted. An allowance for continued research is built into the computations. If the result suggests that the extension of the patent is necessary to provide a price for the manufacturer that will cover continuation of research at the prior patent period level, it is a powerful argument for granting the patent. On the other hand, if the lower price that the manufacturer could obtain under unprotected market competition would suffice to support continued research, it is a powerful argument against an extension.

An overview such as that suggested above conforms to marginalist theory in that it looks to the future, not the past. Sunk investment costs as such are disregarded. But in their place an allowance for continued research in the future is substituted. This trade-off is about as far in the direction of historical regulatory considerations as the patent-extension process should go.

The foregoing alternative has been framed in terms of its application to consideration of a drug patent extension. Suitably modified, it also might apply to software.

Final Thoughts

The alternatives listed above cover a range of possible applications of "special case" marginalist concepts. The list is intended to be suggestive, not exclusive.

A marginalist approach is superior to an averaged approach because it isolates the future result of the specific change under study. Composited studies, on the other hand, particularly if focused on overall results over past periods, tend to dilute the future impact of the change. Therefore, the marginal approach is superior when the objective is to evaluate the result of a change in conditions. Mergers and patent extensions illustrate studies having this type of objective.

Other objectives are more general in nature, such as those related to the measurement of the value of research in the New Economy.

Other than mergers, there has been no attempt to identify specific possibilities for using the methodology in antitrust and FTC issues. It should be helpful on issues where the reasonableness of future prices under alternative circumstances might be the subject of controversy. For these, the base approach might be sufficient, or special case modifications might be required. There is no intent to limit the ingenuity of the analyst to the approaches mentioned. The analyst is invited to expand, and, by all means, to improve.

The foregoing pages frequently refer to the prices and supplies of prescription drugs, which are viewed as major issues facing the New Economy at this time. In the real world, these issues appear in many different guises, ranging from patent disputes to inter-company conflicts for market share. Impacting circumstances vary from one event to another.

7. Antitrust

The Great Antitrust Debate:
Focus on Innovation?
Or Stick to Pricing Issues?
The Outcome Is Critical.
—Business Week, *June 26, 2000*

The Statutes in General

The Antitrust Laws are predicated upon the preservation and enhancement of competition, and the correlative, the prevention of monopoly.

The Sherman Act (1890) forbids actions in restraint of trade (contracts, combinations, and conspiracies) as well as monopolization and attempts to monopolize. The Clayton Act (1914) is more specific, defining antitrust violations and prohibiting price discrimination that substantially lessens competition or creates a monopoly (as well as other actions that might have the same result, including contracts that prevent buyers from dealing with seller's competitors; tying contracts; acquisition of one corporation's shares of stock by another that would substantially lessen competition; and interlocking directorates between competitors). The Robinson-Patman Act (1936) adds another specific regarding price discrimination. It prohibits charging different prices to different customers for goods that are essentially similar in grade and

Acknowledgment: I am grateful to Diarmuid F. O'Scannlain, U.S. Circuit Judge for the Ninth Circuit, U.S. Court of Appeals, for his review and helpful comments on this chapter. Judge O'Scannlain is not responsible for any errors that remain, or for the recommendation made, which are my sole responsibilities.

quality, where the effect would be a substantial lessening of competition or a tendency toward monopoly. Price discrimination is permitted only if (1) it is based on cost differences; (2) it meets competition in good faith; or (3) it is based upon the perishability or obsolescence of a product. Finally, the Cellers-Kefauver Act (1950) strengthens the law against anticompetitive mergers by prohibiting acquisitions by competitors of assets (as well as of stock), and prohibiting mergers if an industry shows a trend toward concentration.

In 1914, the year of the enactment of the Clayton Act, the Federal Trade Commission (FTC) was established to investigate "the organization, business conduct, practices and management" of companies in interstate commerce. The commission was instructed to challenge unfair methods of competition and any unfair or deceitful acts or practices of these companies. As a consequence, the antitrust laws are enforced by the FTC and the Antitrust Division of the Department of Justice, with the courts as the ultimate authority on contested issues.

The genesis of the laws is explained in the 2001 joint DeLong-Summers paper:

> . . . political changes—the rise of antitrust—were needed for two reasons. The first was to try to make sure that the enormous economies of scale within the grasp of the large corporation were not achieved at the price of replacing competition by monopoly. The second was the political function of reassuring voters that the growing large corporations would be the economy's servants rather than the voters' masters.

Twin Principles

The laws clearly establish the twin principles that competition is good and monopoly is bad. They do not spell out the reasons why competition is good, however. The microeconomist is likely to suggest that the benefit of competition is that it leads to "competitive prices," which are taken to be prices to consumers that are as low as practicable in a free economy. Monopoly, the absence of competition, may result in prices higher than they would be in a competitive market. Therefore, because of the price disadvantage to consumers, monopoly should be prevented in favor of competition. This line of reasoning suggests that the aim of the antitrust laws is to encourage a market environment that will induce low prices and discourage market conditions that may result in higher prices. If this is the aim of the laws, although unexpressed directly, then prices became a linchpin for antitrust judgments. Marginal costs, the subject of this book, point to the normative methodology, which could be a pattern for price evaluations. However, interpretations of the laws are complex and extend far beyond the narrow scope of this book, which focuses on the single element of cost/price determination. Leaving to others an examination of these other extensive elements of antitrust, this chapter is confined to a few observations.

Few would doubt that the antitrust statutes stem from the legacy of Adam Smith's "invisible hand." Competition moves the hand in the right direction, toward the interests of society, and any action that interferes with competition obstructs that movement. However, Smith did not extend his rationale to establish a link between the interests of society in general and appropriate prices in particular. That link seems to be inferred, rather than expressed.

Relative to theory, generalized economics does not attempt to prove that competition will result in the lowest prices to consumers (except in the theoretical case of "perfect" competition), or that monopoly will necessarily result in higher prices (except in the theoretical case of "perfect monopoly"). These two polar cases are not significant in the real world, if they exist at all.[1] The middle and prevailing ground is "monopolistic (or imperfect) competition." Here, for example, product differentiation arising from brand promotion can give the producer an element of monopoly power until competitors enter the market with an equally appealing product at a comparable cost and price.[2] Such monopoly power is temporary insofar as it is postulated that competitors have freedom of entry.

These economic references are vague guidelines at best, and fall far short of providing insight into the determination of relevant levels of prices, particularly for the New Economy.

The antitrust laws themselves are equally vague regarding price levels. In fact, they are stated in the subjective mode: price discrimination that would substantially lessen competition or create a monopoly; or price differentiation for like products that would have the same effects. These standards leave unanswered the question of how prices are to be measured to determine whether unlawful discrimination or differentiation exists. In fact, left open is any suggestion about the extent of price differences that are substantial enough to impair competition and lead to monopoly.

Price Is a Slippery Standard

The courts have struggled with this gap. How are price differences to be measured? It is recognized that a price itself, an absolute amount, does not point to whether it is too high, too low, or just right. (This deficiency applies whether the price stands alone or is compared with other prices.)

With respect to motivation, a price reflects the net of a host of influences in the mind of the seller at the time it is set, some of which are demand related, others supply related. These influences are variable, not fixed, and may change from moment to moment. In other words, today's price may represent fairly the combination of motives that were in the seller's mind when it was set yesterday, but which may no longer apply today and certainly will have been superseded by tomorrow.

By the same token, the mix of motivations behind the price of one seller cannot reasonably be expected to match the motivations of a competitor. In other words, the prices of sellers are not comparable in terms of original intent, except by happenstance.

It is true that the economic function of price is the same for all sellers, namely, to recover in price all of the seller's costs, including as high a level of profit as the market will permit. (In the long term, in equilibrium, the prevailing profit level may be expressed as the "normal" level, but this hardly clarifies any actual price, because no seller knows what the normal level is.) This simple statement of function does not explain price differences.

To explore price differences, it is necessary to explore the cost differences that underlie them. The courts have reached a prevailing view on this matter only with respect to predatory pricing. Here the view is that the proper baseline measure is average variable cost. Specifically, in the view of many courts, predatory pricing occurs when a firm prices a product below its average variable cost. It is cautioned, however, that this issue has not been settled definitively.

Variable cost is the same as short-run marginal cost, which is the minimum cost that must be covered by price if the product or service is not to be sold at an out-of-pocket loss. This minimum includes no profit, and no allowance for fixed investment costs that do not vary with output. A price set at short-run marginal cost is a nonsustainable price, for a business cannot remain a going concern if fixed costs fail to be recovered over an extended period.

Because a marginal cost-based price is a minimum price, sustainable only in the short run, it is appropriate to hold that any price below this level must be predatory. Why else, other than to inhibit competition, would a seller price its product at an out-of-pocket loss? Beyond the predatory pricing cost standard, there is little to go on regarding methods of testing the reasonableness of price in an antitrust context.

It is argued extensively below that the purpose of the antitrust laws is to assure reasonable prices for consumers, or, as Judge Bork puts it in broader terms, to enhance consumer welfare. Reasonable prices for consumers, and thus consumer welfare in general, can be brought into play in antitrust enforcement by adopting the principle that *an appropriate recovery of costs is the economic standard for a reasonable price*. This standard, by focusing on reasonable cost recovery, makes it unnecessary to attempt to evaluate prices as absolute amounts with intent as a criterion.[3]

Recommended Application

This chapter suggests that the principles of marginalism, applied in the predatory standard, be extended with suitable modifications to apply also in other antitrust matters where the testing of price is applicable.

The Bork Viewpoint

Competitive Prices, the Antitrust Goal

A fundamental premise of chapter 6 and this chapter is that the implicit, although unstated, aim of the antitrust laws is to maintain competitive-level prices to consumers. This premise is the link between antitrust and marginalism. The link is no better established than in the views of Robert H. Bork, judge, distinguished scholar, and economist, as explained in his early book, *The Antitrust Paradox*. The *Paradox* is quoted extensively under this heading without further attribution.[4] Bork does not identify competitive-level pricing as the aim of the antitrust laws. He substitutes a broader measure, "the welfare of consumers."[5] The liberty is taken, however, of translating Bork's consumer welfare standard as a pragmatic equivalent to maintaining a system of fully competitive prices, such prices being the means by which consumer interests are protected. In this respect, it is pointed out that the statutory language directly prohibits pricing actions that would (or could) result in noncompetitive prices. It is also pointed out that, in normative terms, price is the tangible signal that, by directing the buying choices of consumers, points toward or away from economic efficiency. Economic efficiency is reached only by fully competitive prices.

After reciting in meticulous detail the deficiencies he sees in the direction that antitrust enforcement has taken—deficiencies that have arisen in his view because of errors in applying economic principles—Bork recommends:

1. The only goal that should guide interpretation of the antitrust laws is the welfare of consumers. Departures from that standard destroy the consistency and predictability of the law; run counter to the legislative intent, as that intent is conventionally derived; and damage the integrity of the judicial process by involving the courts in grossly political choices for which neither the statutes nor any other acceptable source provide any guidance.

2. In judging consumer welfare, productive efficiency, the single most important factor contributing to that welfare, must be given due weight along with allocative efficiency. Failure to consider productive efficiency—or worse, the tendency to view it as pernicious by calling it a "barrier to entry" or a "competitive advantage"—is probably the major reason for the deformation of antitrust's doctrines. (405)

Bork's definitions of allocative and productive efficiencies are included in chapter 6.[6] Note that the equivalency of his consumer welfare standard to the price standard stated earlier herein is borne out by the references in (2) above. Only a lower price could be construed as a barrier to entry or as conferring a competitive advantage. A higher price would be the reverse—an invitation to entry and a competitive disadvantage.

But what price or prices? The answer varies with the context of the question.

For example, if seller A's price is 80 cents per unit, and competitive seller B's price is $1.00 per unit (presumably the lowest price that B can offer and still stay in business), is the lower price predatory, a barrier to entry, conferring a competitive advantage? Marginal cost pricing theory would answer, we do not know. A simple comparison of the two prices does not suffice. But the theory provides the methodology, outlined in chapter 3, by which an answer can be reached. If the cost analysis for A shows that A's marginal costs are equal to or lower than its price, 80 cents per unit is validated. The normative position that optimal price should approach marginal costs has been satisfied. Presumably, the lower price results from operational efficiencies. If, however, A's costs are higher than 80 cents per unit, indicating that it was selling at a loss, an opposite conclusion might be called for. The burden of proof would fall upon A to justify circumstances that required a loss price.

The above simple example goes to the very heart of normative economics. Prices should be evaluated in terms of the marginal costs that they represent. Prices are not abstract numbers that can be accepted at face value: underlying costs must be examined.

Much of the *Antitrust Paradox* relates to a critique of the theories followed by the U.S. Supreme Court in resolving antitrust matters. Most of these involve legal intricacies supported by the Court's current interpretations of its earlier decisions. Only selected opinions of Bork that are relevant to price as a tool in antitrust are mentioned.

The Conflicting Goals

It has been pointed out earlier that Bork's antitrust goal of consumer welfare can be interpreted as being substantially equivalent to the goal of a "competitive price." Bork challenges the alternative goal of small business welfare that has sometimes been favored by the Court. He sees this as being in direct conflict with the goal of consumer welfare. He claims that preferences for small businesses are hostile to competition because such preferences operate to protect the inefficient firm from [price] competition.

In broader terms, Bork views the conflicting goals as "special forms of larger ideas contending for domination in the society at large—toward concern for group rather than general welfare and toward a vague but strong egalitarian philosophy" (422).

Trade-Offs

Bork understands that "an antitrust law devoted to consumer welfare faces severe trade-off problems . . . [for example] the destruction of monopoly necessarily involves a sacrifice of business efficiency [although business efficiency benefits consumers]" (79). He elaborates on the trade-off problem as the clash between welfare for different societal groups, concluding that resolving the clash is a legislative, not a judicial, function.

> The classic case is the agreement by rivals to fix prices. When this case is brought before a court for a determination of legality, there is a head-on conflict between consumer and producer interests. Consumers would prefer a competitive price, that is, a decision that the price-fixing agreement is illegal per se. Producers would prefer a monopoly price, that is, a decision that they may agree upon any price they choose. The court can obtain a clear rule for decision making by choosing to be guided entirely by either group's welfare, though to choose producer welfare as the sole guide is forbidden by the entire thrust of the antitrust laws. But if the court attempts to give weight to both values, to arbitrate a price between the competitive and the monopolistic, it will find that there are no criteria whatever to guide its decision. By deciding what price the cartel may charge, the court decides how much each of the two groups "deserves" at the expense of the other. The judge can relate the decision to nothing more objective than his own sympathies or political views.
>
> The problem differs in detail but not in principle in merger cases such as *Brown Shoe*, where the Supreme Court's objection was that the creation of new efficiencies threatened some rivals with a diminution of their market shares or, possibly, with extinction. The Court has not chosen to ignore the benefits of efficiency completely, or it would tolerate no mergers at all. Here the consumer interest favors the merger and the efficiency, as does the interest of the merged firms; the interest of other producers, at least those not capable of achieving similar efficiencies, is in having the merger declared illegal and dissolved. There is no danger of monopoly profit, but the opposition of interest groups is the same as in the price-fixing case, and there are again no objective criteria for striking a balance between them. Striking the balance is essentially a legislative task. (80)

Theory and Models

Bork's opinions rely heavily on price theory, and its use of models. He outlines the broad classification of differing market structures found in the economy as described in conventional economic models.

> I will sketch the most basic aspects of the conventional theories of competition, monopoly, and oligopoly. Each of these terms describes an

industry structure. Economic theory attempts to relate structure to performance, and performance to the goal of consumer welfare. The theories are listed in descending order of rigor. The theory of competition states the way in which firms *must* behave if they are to survive when the market is competitively structured. The theory of monopoly states the way in which a firm possessing control of a market *can* behave in order to maximize profits. Conventional oligopoly theory, however, is little more than a guess about the ways in which firms might be able to behave in a market composed of a few sellers. (92)

Every economist at one time or another has struggled with the benefits and the limitations of these models. Bork's thoughts on this score are of interest.

The economist's models of competition and monopoly are descriptive. The lawyer's, if he thinks of antitrust as designed to preserve competition and destroy monopoly, must be normative. There is a wide gap in practical consequences. The economist builds a pure model in order to clarify thought; such models are indispensable starting places for policy analysis, but they are not prescriptions for policy. They leave out too much. A determined attempt to remake the American economy into a replica of the textbook model of competition would have roughly the same effect on national wealth as several dozen strategically placed nuclear explosions. To say that is not to denigrate the models but to warn against their misuse. (92)

Price Discrimination

Bork shows deep concern over the enforcement of the price discrimination features of Robinson-Patman. He feels that enforcement has "dealt half-heartedly and ineffectively with price differences." He says:

Though the statute speaks of price discrimination, it is settled that the act merely means price difference. The distinction is important. Price discrimination in the economic sense occurs when a seller realizes different rates of return on sales of the same product to different purchasers. (Another way of saying the same thing is that a seller who discriminates charges different purchasers prices that are proportionally unequal to his marginal costs.) It is thus clear that price *difference does not necessarily involve price discrimination, and price identity does not rule out discrimination.* Since the triggering event for Section 2(a) is a price difference, the statute simply ignores economic discrimination when prices are the same. (383, emphasis added)

Bork contends that enforcement has needlessly deformed market processes by altering legitimate pricing decisions because of the fear of the act: quantity discounts and discounts of other kinds, promotional allowances, and so forth. The fear arises because of the difficulty of framing a cost justification for price differences.

The joint DeLong-Summers paper sees price discrimination differently and urges a more lenient approach for the New Economy. The paper states:

> For most of the past century price discrimination—charging one price to one set of consumers and a very different price for a nearly identical product to another set of consumers—has been viewed by most as an unmixed evil. It has been seen as a way that those with monopoly power can further increase their monopoly profits. But price discrimination has another face as well: it is a way that businesses can extend their market and make their product of more value to consumers. An information good-providing firm that successfully engages in price discrimination can still make a profit by charging high prices to its relatively well-off core market, and can add to that profit and greatly increase the social utility of its product by charging low prices to those who are relatively poor. It may well be that in the information age our attitude toward price discrimination should shift.
>
> There are many cases—of which the provision of pharmaceuticals to people living in poor countries is only the most critical and obvious—in which good public policy should focus on making it easier for companies to charge wildly different prices to different groups of consumers. . . . Effective ways of segmenting the market more completely, so that rich country customers could pay the fixed costs while poor country customers paid close to marginal cost, has the potential to create an enormous addition to world welfare.

Cartels

Bork asserts that "the subject of cartels lies at the center of antitrust policy. The law's oldest and, properly qualified, most valuable rule states that it is illegal per se for competitors to agree to limit rivalry among themselves" (266). The qualification he mentions are circumstances where price fixing and market division are beneficial, as they may be when the agreement is ancillary to cooperative productive activity by the agreeing parties (i.e., when the effect of the agreement does not restrict output).

Efficiency

Bork discounts claims that advertising may be a barrier to entry. In doing so, he makes this interesting point on efficiency.

> Efficiency does not arise solely from cutting costs. It also arises from offering products that people want more, even if those products cost more to produce. It is wrong to say that the Mustang is produced more efficiently than the Lincoln Continental because it costs less. Raising average costs through promotional and informational expenditures is not different from raising average costs through expenditures on larger engines. Both are efficient and procompetitive if consumers like them. (319)

Marginal Cost

Bork appears to be pessimistic about the use of marginal cost as a yardstick. In one comment he says: " . . . in a price fixing case, for example, the court would first have to measure the gap between price and marginal cost—in itself an almost impossible task" (114). At a different point, he elaborated in relation to a larger firm making several products and operating in distinct product and geographic markets:

> This would mean the study of not one but a number of technical marginal cost curves. For each of these, one would face the complex problem of separating fixed and variable costs and the insoluble problem of segregating and allocating joint costs. These things can be and are done by artificial accounting conventions, but that process, however useful it may be to a firm that wishes to compare its own performance during two different time periods, has little validity for the issues of real costs that antitrust policy must decide. Moreover, real marginal costs include a "normal" return to the various resources employed which includes opportunity costs, the latter being the return various resources could earn in the most profitable alternative use in the economy. (127)

Bork also expresses reservations about a rule such as: "A monopolist or any large established firm pricing below marginal cost should be presumed to have engaged in a predatory or exclusionary practice." He also argues against substituting average variable cost, presumably but not accurately shown in conventional business accounts, as a proxy for marginal cost (154).

Bork's critique of marginal costs has been included because these costs have been adopted as a yardstick for evaluation in chapters 5 and 6, and for the discussion of various scenarios in the concluding pages of this chapter. It would be inexcusable to rely on Bork when his views advance the thesis proposed herein, and to ignore him when his views are contrary.

There is no disagreement with Bork over his contention that there are formidable obstacles in the marginal cost approach. In fact, some of the obstacles of marginal costing are highlighted herein, with particular reference to the difficulties of ascertaining costs for a multiproduct firm. But these obstacles are not impossible to surmount, and it is worth the effort.

The Cost Standard

Broadly speaking, a price that recovers the seller's costs (including a reasonable or "normal" profit) has economic validity and has passed the economic test. If a price exceeds this standard, perhaps by reason of an excessive profit, it remains suspect as *possibly* unduly monopolistic; or, if it falls short, it remains suspect as *possibly* predatory.

This cost standard is deceptively simplistic. For example, it fails to highlight the difficulty of determining the appropriate booked costs to be included, appropriate adjustments thereto, as well as nonbooked costs such as profit. To avoid overstatement, some specific cost (supply-side) uncertainties are mentioned below, distinguishing between costing for a single-product firm and a multiproduct firm.

Single-Product Firms

For a competitive single-product firm (whose products are identical or essentially so), cost differences per unit of product from one firm to another will arise because of different costs of production (reflecting scale and operational efficiencies, plant loadings, labor costs, etc.) as well as differences in profit levels. No two suppliers will be entirely alike in these respects. Adjustment of booked production costs might be indicated to place output levels of comparative firms on a uniform basis. A further difference could arise because one of the firms computed its operational costs on a marginal basis (i.e., as the change in costs occurring because of a change in output or scope, regardless of embedded costs), while the other computed its average costs, including embedded costs, each firm making the computation as a basis for its price. Resulting prices would be quite different, although each computation was rational. In any event, comparison of the two raw costs would be an apples-and-oranges combination in any antitrust review. As a minimum, a uniform cost basis would have to be adopted to make the costs comparable. (The marginal cost basis is strongly recommended, but that is beside the point.)

Multiproduct Firms

Per-unit product cost determinations for the multiproduct firm include the same uncertainties as for the single-product firm, but with an additional huge complication. This arises from the illusive nature of a cost calculation for an individual product produced in common with other products, as is the case in varying degrees for all multiproduct firms. The analyst can be certain only about *direct* costs (those incurred solely for the given product). *Indirect*, or common, costs must be spread among the common products on the basis of some subjective, judgmental formula, with the result that the final total cost associated with each individual product is partially estimated. This applies whether the cost basis is marginal or average.

Price comparisons, of course, involve two or more prices. This means that any cost justification for one comparative price must be comparable in terms of cost-determining methodology (including allocation methods) with that used for the others. This comparability requirement compounds the work of the analyst.

Overall, the multiproduct firm will endeavor to recover its total costs, including profit, through its composite revenues. It does not differ from the single-product firm in this respect. But beyond recovery of combined *total* costs, it is unlikely that the typical firm pays much attention to allocation of common costs among individual products as a pricing guide. Individual product prices are more likely to be set on the basis of what the market will bear, irrespective of cost allocations.

This is not to infer that costs are disregarded by the multiproduct firm. Attention will be given to the reduction of direct costs, and it would be unusual (if not irrational) if a product price was insufficient to cover the product's direct costs. Most attention will be given to reducing the major components of common costs, such as wages, input materials, factory schedules, efficiency measures, and the like, without concern about how these may eventually be allocated.

It thus is concluded that the link is imperfect between a product's market price and the allocated cost of the product, especially if it has been produced in common with other products.

On the demand side, the profit margin that the seller can safely include in a price is a major uncertainty because of the seller's lack of firm knowledge of competitors' future prices (assuming no collusion, of course). Market share, increasing it or retaining it, may be another uncertainty. Launching a new or improved product may suggest different price relationships than those for an existing product. The state of the economy as a whole may play a role. The list of price-influencing demand factors goes on and on. It is concluded that any given price of a seller, or any such price in comparison with the price of a competitor, is subject to so many uncertainties as to make unreliable any guess regarding the seller's potpourri of motivations, whether the seller is plaintiff or defendant in the antitrust action.

Because price is the means by which the seller recovers its costs, including profit, the legitimacy of a suspect price (absent illegal collusion) rests upon the reasonableness of the relationship of price to cost. This suggestion avoids attempting to analyze price in the abstract (i.e., as a composite of the seller's motivations); rather, it bypasses intent, going directly to the underlying costs.

From the buyer's viewpoint, price is the measure of the drain on his or her pocketbook for obtaining a product. Here again, the question regarding a suspect price is whether that drain is reasonable or otherwise, which can be answered only in terms of the costs of producing the product.

Is Costing Worthwhile?

The obvious question is whether it is worthwhile and an improvement to adopt comparative costs as an antitrust yardstick.

Antitrust questions regarding price (as distinct from questions regarding monopolistic practices) arise because the reasonableness of a seller's price has come under question as being possibly in violation of the antitrust statutes. The price may stand alone as being violative per se, or be suspect because of its relationship to other relevant prices charged by competing sellers, or both. In either case, the issue boils down, in essence, to proof of the economic validity of the suspect price.

A price alone, say $1.00 per unit,[7] tells nothing other than that the product has been offered for sale at $1.00. Further information may show that the offer has been accepted by "x" buyers or none. Comparative prices tell nothing in addition except that a competing seller(s) has offered a similar product at, say, $1.50 per unit, with "y" units sold, if any.

One can only guess as to the motivations—or more likely the series of motivations—that influenced the individual seller in arriving at its price. Was the economy improving, so that pushing a luxury product might pay off, or was it deteriorating, so that a necessity-type product would be more salable? Was quality or service an issue, so that the seller felt it necessary to lower its price to lure customers to accept its possibly inferior product, or conversely, felt it safe to increase its price because the public perception was that it offered a superior product? Were competitors advertising aggressively? Was demand strong or weak?

Did the seller's factory have excess capacity, making it prudent to stimulate sales volumes even at a reduced price? Was the market in general saturated with capacity or short of capacity? Any of these could explain price differences.

Or, was a competitor threatening to erode the seller's market share, inducing the seller to attempt to drive the competitor out of the market by a cutthroat price?

Price alone gives no insight into these questions. There is no tangible solid basis for support of, or opposition to, the validity of a price except as inferences regarding motive may be introduced. Cost, in contrast, is tangible and relatively solid, although there are uncertainties in cost calculations, particularly for a product produced in common.

The two *Business Week* questions cited at the beginning of this chapter are now discussed, with the second question addressed first.

Stick to Pricing Issues? Applicability of Marginal Cost Techniques to Traditional Issues

Mergers may be examined from perspectives other than antitrust. Utility mergers, for example, are subject to Federal Energy Regulatory Commission and state regulatory commission approval. For this reason, mergers were discussed in chapter 6 rather than here.

As outlined in chapter 6, marginalist methodology is well suited for the evaluation of research, the probable source of most future innovation. In this sense the methodology fits the New Economy and is pertinent to Summers's message. But his message goes well beyond research, as will be discussed later under "Focus on Innovation?"

Chapter 6 also explained how the marginalist approach might be used to resolve a drug patent extension application. However, that explanation does not extend to consideration of the possibility that the patent extension might be a cause of delay in introducing an equivalent generic drug: It assumed the existence of the generic drug. A motivation to delay a new competing product adds intent to the analysis (as intent may be a factor in predatory pricing). The methodology does not presume to measure *intent*. Similarly, it does not presume to detect collusion between competitors, whether that collusion is motivated toward a better price or toward delaying innovation. *Detection* is well beyond the scope of this book.

Nevertheless, despite its inability to detect unlawful circumstances, the marginal cost approach could be a helpful tool in resolving several types of antitrust issues. Four simple scenarios are sketched below to illustrate.

Scenario One: Price Collusion (Constant Plant Condition; Uncontested Data)

The method could be used as a guide to whether a suspect price had been raised to reflect higher costs, a legitimate reason, or, alternatively, might have been raised as a result of collusion among competitors, an antitrust violation. Cost/price differences before and after the suspected wrongful act could be compared. Comparison of abstract prices alone would not suffice. A more valid comparison requires the price as it would be without the suspected act to be juxtaposed with the price as it was after the act. Both costs would be determined on a marginal cost basis.

For example, assume that the earlier price (before collusion) was $1.00 per unit, and the later price (after the alleged collusion) was $1.05 per unit. Simple arithmetic might be taken to suggest that collusion raised prices by 5 cents per unit. With a sales volume of 10 million units, the consumer now is paying $500,000 more than formerly. However, the arithmetic answer may be too simple because cost levels for both prices are disregarded. Illustrated below is how cost might be introduced in the marginalist fashion to imply either collusion or its absence (or at least, the absence of any detriment to consumers).

The table below adopts the above price relationships to illustrate how the methodology might suggest one result or the other. Plant is assumed to remain unchanged. The data are assumed to be uncontested.

| | Scenario One | | |
| | Before suspicion of collusion (a) | Alternative suspect conditions | |
		(b)	(c)
Price	$1.00	$1.05	$1.05
Marginal cost	0.65	0.70	0.65
Excess available for fixed costs	0.35	0.35	0.40

Column (b) suggests that the price increase is justified insofar as it merely reflects an equivalent increase in costs. On the other hand, column (c) suggests that the increase in price may be questionable insofar as it raises the marginal excess without any change in the marginal costs of production.

Scenario Two: Price Collusion (Added Plant Condition; Challenges to Data)

This scenario introduces the possibility that plant may be added in an effort to reduce marginal production costs, a common occurrence. So that the reader need not resort to a calculator, it is assumed that the marginal increase in investment for the new plant is $10 million, with an annual carrying cost of about 9 percent to 10 percent. With the same production level of $10 million units, the per unit additional marginal investment costs would range from 9 cents per unit to 10 cents. (The carrying cost is likely to be at least double, probably exceeding 20 percent if taxes are included.)

Scenario Two also drops the major assumption that the marginal costs are accepted as accurate. Here they are subject to challenge. The situation is now adversarial. It is assumed that columns (a) and (b) in the table below have been advanced by the company under review. Column (c) has been offered by an opposing party, either the regulatory staff or an intervenor.

| | Scenario Two | | |
| | Before suspicion of collusion (a) | Alternative suspect conditions | |
		(b)	(c)
Price	$1.00	$1.05	$1.05
Marginal cost			
Production	0.65	0.60	0.56
Investment		0.10	0.09
Excess available for fixed costs	0.35	0.35	0.40

Column (a) is the same base condition as was the starting point for Scenario One. In columns (b) and (c), marginal production costs are assumed to be reduced by reason of the addition of efficient plant, resulting in production cost savings that are offset, in whole or part, by the increase in marginal investment costs because of the added plant.

The opposing party agrees with the company that column (a) is valid and acceptable as a starting point, but strongly disagrees with column (b), arguing that column (c) reflects more accurate data. The opposing party contends that production line efficiencies have reduced marginal production costs to 56 cents per unit (not to just 60 cents as held by the company) and that investment efficiencies result in marginal investment costs of 9 cents per unit (not the company's higher 10 cents). Its figures, the opposing party says, show that collusion has permitted the company to raise its price and its profit by 5 cents per unit.

The company vigorously defends its column (b) data. It denies any collusion and argues that the increase in its price is sufficient only to cover its higher costs. The company points out that its decision to add plant has been demonstrated to be reasonable because that has kept its marginal costs to preexisting levels except for inflation.

Which is right? Offhand, this cannot be answered because the data are in conflict. This conflict forces the regulatory body (the FTC or the Antitrust Division of the U.S. Department of Justice) independently to examine the company's books to determine and adopt a set of marginal costs that is valid in its opinion.

This controversy is added in Scenario Two to point out the fact that the marginalist approach, while forthright in principle, is not necessarily as clear-cut in result as it might seem. The test is the accuracy of the cost data upon which the calculations rest. (Recall that Bork questions the analyst's ability to develop accurate data.)

Scenario Three: Predatory Pricing

This scenario posits a different condition. It illustrates possibilities that could occur in a predatory pricing proceeding in which a price is suspect as being too low. Specifically, it is assumed that firm A has been accused of selling below cost.

In terms of theory, the allegation could not rest upon a showing that the suspect price is below *average* cost. Many products are sold below average cost through reasonable and lawful price discrimination. The allegation would have to prove that the suspect price is below *marginal* cost.

The marginal costs of accused firm A might fit into one of three patterns. For each pattern it can be assumed that the price is $1.00 per unit. This price is uncontested. A contends that its market for the product is a sales volume of 1 million units, resulting in revenues of $1 million. A further contends that its marginal costs total $1 million. From these contentions, it draws the conclusion that price equals marginal cost and is therefore validated. (Summers, "under competition, price can sink to marginal costs.") The proof A offers is simple.

A's Contention: Sales of 1 Million Units Marginal Costs = $1 million		
	Marginal Costs	
	Total	Per unit
Revenues	$1,000,000	$1.00
Marginal costs	1,000,000	1.00
Excess or loss	0	0

A's proof is subject to challenge in two directions: First, it may be charged that the sales volume is overstated, that it should be 900,000 units rather than 1 million, presenting the following revision.

Sales Volume Challenge: Sales of 900,000 units Marginal Costs = $1 million		
	Marginal Costs	
	Total	Per unit
Revenues	$ 900,000	$1.00
Marginal costs	1,000,000	1.11
Excess or loss	($100,000)	($0.11)

This version accepts that total marginal costs are $1 million in total, but calculates marginal costs per unit to be $1.11 with a smaller volume of production.

A more sweeping challenge could allege that not only has the volume been overstated, as above, but in addition that marginal costs have been understated.

Volume and Cost Challenge: Sales of 900,000 Units Marginal Cost = $1.1 million		
	Marginal Costs	
	Total	Per unit
Revenues	$ 900,000	$1.00
Marginal costs	1,100,000	1.22
Excess or loss	($200,000)	($0.22)

The possibilities of challenges to the numbers are introduced above to underscore, once again, the importance of accurate input data, some of which may be judgmental.

Absent circumstances over and above costing accuracy, A's evidence, if it stood up under challenge, would be strong economic support for the lawfulness of its price. It was not selling at a loss in order to undermine competitors or gain any unlawful advantage. On the other hand, if the challenger's volume or marginal cost data were to be adopted as more accurate, firm A's price might be suspect as predatory because sales below cost are suggested. These are not firm conclusions even from the economic point of view. Factors other than the cost/price relationship shift might be as important. A judge's decision is difficult to predict.

To the point, Scenario Three has postulated conditions of selling at or below marginal costs. But selling above marginal costs might also be questioned, if the excess over marginal costs was deemed to be too small judged by prevailing industry standards. In an earlier chapter it was pointed out that the predicate for the "price = marginal cost" equation rests upon the assumptions of the perfect competition model, which are rarely if ever realized in full in the actual economy. Some excess would seem to be the norm.

Three patterns might be found, with marginal costs decreasing and excess increasing from one to the other.

	Patterns		
	(1)	(2)	(3)
Price	$1.00	$1.00	$1.00
Marginal costs	0.95	0.50	0.25
Excess	0.05	0.50	0.75

The first pattern shows a condition where marginal costs comprise almost the entirety of the price, with only a nominal excess for the coverage of fixed costs. The second pattern portrays a condition where marginal costs and the excess comprise equal portions of the price, and the third, where the excess is the largest portion of the price. The existence of *any* excess reflects a lack of equilibrium, a departure from the pure competition model; it suggests the prevalent condition of monopolistic competition. Can marginalist methodology be a useful tool for evaluation of predatory pricing in this circumstance?

The answer is a "qualified yes."

Firms having a large research base are disregarded in this answer, having discussed research-type firms in chapter 6 as a "special case."

Earlier it has been stated that a full traditional utility-type determination of a reasonable price should be avoided because of its practical difficulties and also because the problem is not to determine a regulated price. Yet some yardstick to measure the validity of the excess is necessary to evaluate any of the three patterns (and, indeed, might be necessary for the illustrations in Scenarios One and Two as well).

As a reasonable yardstick, the average excess experience of a group of representative (namely, similar) firms in the concerned industry might be used. The excess would be expressed as a percentage of the price. The percentage of the high and low firms within the group would give the range of the several percentages comprising the average experience. The possibility of calculating such a yardstick is the reason for the "qualified yes."

It would be speculative to presume to prejudge the weight that would be given to the yardstick in any given circumstance. Assume that the composite experience of similar firms showed that half of the price was for the coverage of fixed costs (coinciding with the second pattern). For pattern (1), for example, the defendant supporting this pattern could argue that, despite the group experience, its price was vindicated because marginal costs were more than recouped in full. The plaintiff might argue that a 50 percent coverage of fixed costs was too low, and that the defendant actually was selling at a loss. These conflicting arguments would present to the court the clear choice between two divergent economic models—pure competition versus monopolistic competition.

Scenario Four: Monopoly Pricing

If ground is shifted, and it is assumed that a price is being challenged as being too high (a monopoly price, instead of a predatory price that is challenged as being too low), the debate takes a different tone. Assume again that group experience shows a fifty-fifty split in the price between marginal costs and the excess available for fixed costs. This time it is assumed that the suspect price is supported by pattern (3). The challenging party would be expected to argue that any excess for fixed costs above 50 percent is indicative of monopoly. In response the challenged party undoubtedly would attack the validity of the yardstick on a number of grounds (such as questioning the legality of any yardstick under antitrust precedents), the broadest attack; or questioning the representative character of the firms in the sample or the accuracy of the data or other details, a shotgun attack; or advancing a sample of its own that would be more supportive of its position.

The joint paper views monopoly from a more refined perspective, giving DeLong's and Summers's views on the public policies that should govern when the monopoly arises in a situation of high fixed costs and low (near-zero) variable costs. They say:

> An industry with high fixed costs and near-zero variable costs has another important characteristic: it tends to monopoly. The rule-of-thumb in high technology has been that the market leader makes a fortune, the first-runner-up breaks even, and everyone else goes bankrupt rapidly. In such an industrial structure, the only sustainable form of competition becomes competition for the leading position in the next generation market that is growing up now—for competition in already established markets with high fixed and low variable costs is nearly impossible to sustain.
>
> Good public policy in such an environment should make sure that the monopoly profits from the provision of things that become essential services are not too large (although they need to be large to reward all the past investments, successful and failed, in the market). Good public policy in such an environment needs to make sure that producers with a near-monopoly position in one generation's market do not use that position to retard innovation and the growth of the next-generation market, or to guarantee themselves a large head start in the race to establish a leading position in the next-generation market. But good public policy also needs to make sure not to take steps that artificially limit the market shares of the most efficient producers of this generation's products, for larger market shares go with low costs and (relatively) low prices charged to consumers.
>
> It is far from clear how such policies can be designed, or how close policy can get to its ideal, given the blunt instrument that is our legal system.

The Scenarios in Perspective

The preceding four scenarios are not intended to outline full economic proof as to the validity, or lack thereof, of any suspect price, whether the suspicion arises from the possibility of collusion, predatory pricing, or monopoly. Their purpose is limited to suggesting how a marginalist approach might be applied to an examination of costs in support of, or in opposition to, a price under antitrust review. In this narrow perspective, the cost-to-price link shown in the several illustrations might be an informative signal to the direction of an antitrust effort, either toward prosecution or defense. In other words, their purpose is to be a useful guide rather than a case-in-chief.

For all scenarios, additional proof undoubtedly would be required. Taking a monopoly allegation as an example, economic evidence regarding market power, monopolistic practices of the suspect monopolist, the technical nature of the product, the market environment, and other related matters, might overwhelm considerations of price. As observed from newspaper and other media accounts, this seems to be the case in the Microsoft proceeding. So the price-based comparisons to posit in these scenarios might be useful only as supporting indicia, if useful at all.

The first *Business Week* question is now explored.

Focus on Innovation? Summers Revisited

Generally speaking, the law is lethargic, particularly where fundamental principles of public policy are involved. Statutes are resistive to important change, and court decisions interpreting the statutes tend to uphold the precedents established by prior rulings. Yet laws can be changed and new court decisions can supersede earlier ones. Statutory changes and court reversals of earlier positions are, however, at best uphill battles.

Resistance to change would likely be a primary hurdle to be overcome in any serious attempt to adopt Summers's thesis. His temporary monopoly suggestion is aimed at encouraging innovation. Who would object to more innovation in any circumstances, much less when innovation is seen to be uniquely desirable (per conventional wisdom, at least) for the New Economy? If the question is posed in this manner, the answer seems easy. Few would object. But if the question is put in the alternative: Should innovation be substituted for competition as the prime objective of the antitrust laws? The answer is far from clear. As election polls teach us, answers vary with the manner in which the question is framed.

It is not the function of this chapter to attempt to answer this question, regardless of how it may be put. It is concluded only that adoption of temporary monopoly protection to encourage innovation would require an amendment to the antitrust laws, or, as a minimum, a drastic modification of their interpretation by the FTC, the Justice Department, and the courts. The consequences of either would be wide ranging.

For example, if the thrust of antitrust were to shift from preventing monopoly (and higher prices to consumers) to preventing impediments to innovation (disregarding immediate price impacts), the areas of inquiry and burdens of proof would likewise shift. It seems reasonable to conclude that, in any event, "innovation," or what used to be called "creativity," would itself need to be defined and measured in terms of the benefits that were expected to arise therefrom.[8] Many ideas are innovative, but not all are beneficial. The familiar "cost-to-benefit" ratio might need to be applied. The ratio might weigh the costs to society of a temporarily higher price against the perceived longer-term benefits of the innovation.

Assuming a shift in direction toward a "preventing impediments to innovation" approach, antitrust inquiries might examine questions such as whether possible collusion between competitors might be holding up innovations (a *Business Week* question[9]); or whether drug patent extensions might be delaying the introduction of generic drugs; or, turning to the utility industry, whether electric power supply shortages, experienced nationwide during the summer of 2000, resulted from conscious neglect by power generators and transmission companies to invoke innovative techniques that could have alleviated the shortages and thus minimized the much higher electric prices that actually were imposed. Or were these power supply shortages the result of regulatory malfunction?

Innovation itself presents an entirely new list of issues other than those covered in the four scenarios. How new ideas should be encouraged and attempts to block new products discouraged are new public policy issues. Antitrust theory will need to be developed to encompass questions such as these, but that development is beyond the scope of this book. It is pointed out only that it seems inevitable that the twin issues of cost and price, considered in chapter 6 and this chapter, will remain volatile considerations in any new antitrust theory that may evolve. Cost-price implications are ever present.

Utilization of Marginal Costs

Although specifics are illusive, marginalist techniques might be brought into play to resolve issues where promotion of innovation is a dominant antitrust goal. It can only be speculated as to how these techniques might be useful.

Before venturing into this never-never land, it is advisable to try to set forth a foundation. First, any technique is only a means to an end. It is not an end in itself. Second, that end must be defined in terms of policy objectives that seem logical. Only then, with an objective in mind, can an appropriate method of evaluation and measurement be fashioned.

As a broad policy premise, it would seem reasonable that encouragement of competition and discouragement of monopoly would not be dropped as twin antitrust considerations. These would remain in place, but tempered when conflicts arose with the new objective of facilitating innovation. In other words, the emphasis of antitrust enforcement would change somewhat from exclusively preventing monopoly to fostering monopolies in circumstances that encourage innovation.[10]

A more extended use of patents and copyrights immediately comes to mind, because patents and copyrights are embedded in existing law. But these have disadvantages. Although they grant a temporary monopoly and thus provide leeway for the recoupment of prior fixed costs during the patent period (an incentive), they also discourage product improvement innovations over that period by reason of the threat of infringement (a disincentive). (Presumably, an entirely new product would not be disadvantaged by the threat, provided it was clear that it was new, not merely a refinement of a patented product. But the lines of demarcation are likely to be cloudy, particularly for software.) Improvements in the standards for granting and enforcing patents and copyrights seem possible, but these are left to the experts in these fields.

The more difficult conceptual problem is that of meshing competition and innovation, seemingly conflicting, into a set of nonconflicting principles.

Evaluating both competition and innovation should look to the future, at least so it is thought. Normative economics supports this goal. The problem is that no one can predict the future accurately. The future is inherently speculative. Nevertheless, at ground zero, both competition and innovation are prescriptions for the future welfare of society.

The seeming conflict between competition and innovation is real only in the short run. Competition implies no preference to any competitor, so that there will be more and stronger competitors. This is operative in the short run. However, to flourish, innovation may require a degree of protection at the outset, which also must be operative in the short run. Thus, the two short-run objectives conflict. In the longer run, however, they may coexist without conflict, for new ideas lead to new enterprises that are platforms for greater competition. The difficulty is in formulating an antitrust structure that makes the two objectives compatible in the short run.

Many scholars have advocated a compulsory license reform for most patent and copyright protection, whereby intellectual property owners would be forced to allow subsequent inventors to use their inventions in subsequent innovation, but any such use would be compensated by a set royalty. This system already operates with regard to copyrighted musical compositions.

The joint paper adds a cautionary word to the subject of patents. DeLong and Summers say: "Traditional discussions within economics have focused on the length of patents. Yet it may well be that the depth and breadth of patents are at least as important determinants of economic progress."

Letting imagination run riot, sketched out below is a middle-ground proposal that might achieve this compatibility using marginalist principles. The middle ground would employ modest revisions in the antitrust and tax laws to provide a measure of financial protection at an early stage for innovative ventures, but would be short of granting a temporary monopoly. This write-up refers to patents with the understanding that copyrights also might be addressed similarly if appropriate.

An Illustrative Proposal

Objective

To provide a middle ground between full competition and protected patents, so as to encourage innovation with minimum change in existing statutes.

Overview of the Middle Ground

Postponing details other than for the exceptions below, antitrust statutes would remain in place insofar as they outlaw collusion, predatory pricing, and monopoly. Market operations would continue to be monitored as they are now under present law. Likewise, tax laws would not be changed, except to a minor degree.

The *antitrust exception* would expressly permit an innovative firm to include *only* marginal production costs in any evidence it might present as a defense against a predatory pricing accusation. This evidence would conform to marginalist practice for the determination of short-run marginal costs. The absence of costs other than such marginal costs could not be challenged. (The numbers themselves could be challenged, of course, on the basis of accuracy.) The purpose of this provision is to permit the innovative firm to gain a foothold in the market by marginal cost pricing without fear of being accused of selling below cost. Unlike the patent, the innovative firm is not given a temporary monopoly insofar as its processes are not protected. Competitors are free to copy or otherwise take advantage of these processes.

The *income tax exception* would exclude from current taxes any revenues received from the sale of the product, while permitting the inclusion in full, as current expenses, the marginal production costs of the product (including R&D) plus other normal costs. Taxes that otherwise would be owed would be deferred (not forgiven). The main purpose of this temporary tax relief is the same as that for the antitrust exception, namely, to permit a firm to sell its product at a lower price than it otherwise might in order to gain a foothold in the market.

A subsidiary purpose is to recognize that the future flow of capital into innovative ventures may not be as unquestioning as it has been in the past, as entrepreneurs grow more cautious and demand greater expectations of eventual profitability. This tax relief might be attractive to the venture capitalist, encouraging a continued capital inflow for research and development.

These exceptions would not be open-ended. They would extend only to periods established in advance. They also would be accompanied by certain obligations noted below.

Some Details

Unfortunately, but inevitably, statutory changes compel infrastructure changes and require obligations to comport with privileges. This says nothing more than that additional paperwork in the context of the exceptions would be required. This paperwork is designed to be ministerial in nature, rather than regulatory. Several definitions will clarify the paperwork.

An *innovation* is any concept or procedure having potential social value, not under patent or copyright, that an innovative firm wishes to pursue, and for which it has obtained approval pursuant to a "Request for Innovation Incentives." A separate request is required for each innovation, but there is no limit on the number of requests that may be submitted.

The *social value* of the innovation is to be judged mainly in the negative, to rule out any unlawful objective.

Although concepts or procedures under patent or copyright are excluded, improvements in them (e.g., a generic drug to replace a presently patented prescriptive drug, or a new software program to improve an existing patented program) are not excluded.

A written statement by the applicant that the innovation does not conflict with an existing patent or copyright shall be accepted by the receiving agency to make unnecessary any formal patent or copyright review process. This statement does not relieve the applicant of any obligations it might have under patent or copyright law.

Marginalist practices, outlined extensively from a number of different perspectives in this book, embrace, in general, costing that looks to the future rather than the past and measures costs at the margin (incremental costs) rather than average costs.

The major paperwork is a "Request for Innovation Incentives" to be submitted by the applicant firm to designated offices of the FTC, and Justice and Treasury Departments, for approval by whichever of these is designated as lead agency. As mentioned earlier, it is the intent of this proposal that the approval process be ministerial, not regulatory or adversial.

The request would include the following:

(a) A simple description of the proposed project, including a statement of the social benefits that are expected if the project is successful. The purpose of this description is identification only. So long as it is clear, it is not subject to a reasonableness review by the lead agency. The description grants no patent, copyright, or other exclusion that would constrain competitors. However, the description may be submitted under seal to protect proprietary information.

(b) A statement by the applicant that, in its opinion, the project does not infringe upon an existing patent or copyright.

(c) An agreement by the applicant to expend $_____ on research and development or start-up for the project over the period from _____ to _____. Expenditures must be identified with the project on the applicants' books as made. A semiannual or annual report to the lead agency of expenditures made might be required, and an audit by the agency would be permitted. However, progress reports on the project's status, other than a final report, would not be required.

The specified amount to be expended and the project period are key to the antitrust and tax exceptions. These exceptions are granted only for the expenditure amount, and only over the period stated. However, the applicant may request a change in either for due cause.

If ___ percent of the specified amount has not been expended during the specified period, approval of the request will be deemed to have been canceled as of the date of approval. This retroactivity negates any tax benefits that the applicant might have received.

(d) An agreement by the applicant to establish accounting procedures that facilitate the identification of expenditures with the project. If the applicant is an established business, the formation of a subsidiary to pursue the project might be desirable but is not required. In lieu of a subsidiary, the applicant would be required to establish a separate account for the project and define that account in its request. To the extent that common costs may be incurred, as would be expected for a multiproduct business, the applicant would be required to specify the method of allocation of each common cost that it proposes to follow. These allocation methods would be subject to a reasonableness review by the lead agency. It is necessary to agree upon allocation methods at the beginning of the project to eliminate later challenges by either party.

(e) An agreement by the applicant to adhere to marginalist practices in its accounting and reporting on the project.

Epilogue

It approaches the foolhardy to attempt to illustrate an application of marginal cost principles to a new antitrust objective, as has been done above, before the experts in antitrust have studied the objective and formulated the foundational theory that would provide a predicate. It is equally rash to invade the tax laws without an advisory opinion from Treasury or even minimal consultation with tax officials.

These risky steps have been taken in this proposal because otherwise only a broad assertion could have been made to the effect that marginalist principles might be of help in resolving the dilemma of new approaches to innovation. This would have been only a blind assertion, lacking context and demonstration. It is hoped that the proposal provides a degree of context and illustrates a possible linkage between marginal cost methodology and the innovation objective. Nothing more than that is intended. The rest is left to the experts.

8. Concluding Thoughts

The Policy Clash

The Introduction points out the policy clash arising from two opposing views of prices that equate to marginal costs, one view holding that these prices are beneficial, the other that they are detrimental. And it poses the question: Which view is right for the New Economy?

Fortunately, the clash does not present a Hobson's choice, where one must choose one side or the other. Taken in moderation, both views are correct. For example, it is not contradictory to hold that it is good that competition drives prices downward toward marginal costs, while at the same time contending that it would be disastrous if prices as a whole actually fell to that low level. The latter is not likely to occur.

By the same token, it is not contradictory to hold that prices must be adequate to return to the seller all of his invested and out-of-pocket dollars, with profit, while at the same time recognizing that competition often will force prices to be below that adequacy level. For this reason, the application of marginalist methodology varies with the circumstances of the case to which it is directed. In some instances, short-run marginal costs are appropriate (such as for the school voucher study). In other cases, long-run marginal costs are better suited for the objective. The former includes only direct out-of-pocket costs, and the latter, all costs including investment costs. In between are cases where only a part of investment costs are included (such as research and development costs).

Marginalization

This book proposes marginalization as a uniform methodology for the analysis of many ongoing current policy issues, both governmental and corporate. The methodology invokes marginal cost theory and techniques to compare one contemplated policy with another. It focuses on changes at the margin, ignoring changes not directly associated with the policy shift, and states the impact of these changes in terms of future costs and benefits. It is appropriate for a wide range of issues, from isolated unique problems such as school vouchers to multifaceted problems peculiar to antitrust. In other words, the methodology provides a middle ground between the two opposing views on marginal costs.

The Proposed Uniform Approach

For years, policy debates have been clouded by inconsistent and often wildly divergent estimates of the costs of one policy versus another. There has always been a need for consistency in these estimates.

But the need is even greater now, as we enter the twenty-first century, for the Information Age presents a vastly different array of issues to be decided. In many respects these issues are new in nature and more complex in their application.

Now is the time, at long last, to substitute order for chaos insofar as costs are concerned. The proposal made herein for the adoption of marginalism as a uniform approach to cost estimating may be attractive on this score. At the very least, it would provide a common point of departure, giving a measure of consistency to the varying estimates that are likely to be presented. Or, better still, it might establish a basic cost that could be agreed upon as the foundation for argument.

But even if marginalism is not adopted as a method, its foundational thought is valid: There should be consistency in the approach to cost estimating—a common beginning point and uniformity in the calculations. If only this thought takes hold, this book will have been worthwhile.

Appendix
Pre-Kahn Theory
(Bergson, Lerner, Ruggles, and Bonbright)

The writers covered in this appendix outline the origins and evolution of marginal cost pricing theory as it stood prior to Kahn's *Economics*. It provides only a sampling of views on the theory, however, not a compendium. The appendix does not presume to be complete and the choice of authors is perforce selective.

Bergson is placed first as he gives a good introductory overview, embracing the pioneering economists. The other writers appear in chronological order. No attempt has been made to sketch the entirety of the contribution of these other writers. The reviews are confined to early matters of theory that seem to impinge most directly upon the "marginal cost pricing doctrine" as it now stands. So on this score also, they are selective.

As has been done throughout the main text, the writers are quoted in their own language, rather than paraphrased or summarized. For this reason, comments are minimal and are explanatory not analytical.

Abram Bergson: "Socialist Economics," 1949

The Early Writers

Abram Bergson[1] recounts the origins and early development of the "marginal cost pricing doctrine."[2]

Bergson's view is that early writers in this sector of academic thought were focused on ". . . theoretic studies of the economic problems of socialism . . . in the cognate field of welfare economics"[3] (412). Much work centered on the recurring theme of a Central Planning Board—what planning could or should do, or what it could or should not do. A number of writings were concerned "with one large problem: to define the *allocation of resources* that would be an optimum." Bergson notes particularly the pioneering writings of Pareto (1897) and Barone (1908) in the field of *socialist* economics and of Marshall (1890; 1920) and Pigou (1920; 1934) in the field of *welfare* economics (413).

These writers wrestled mightily with the formulation of a "scale of values" for evaluation of the alternative uses of resources. The scale for Marshall and Pigou was the sum of the utilities of the individual households in the community *when incomes are equal*, making the optimum allocation one that maximizes welfare in this sense. The scale of Pareto and Barone was that "it must be impossible by reallocation of resources to enhance the welfare of one household without reducing that of another" (413–14).

An Optimum Allocation

Giving credit to others (including A.P. Lerner's contribution, below*)*, Bergson skips to the mid-twentieth century, presenting "a brief inventory" of conditions required for an *optimum allocation.* The inventory covers conditions that "are either stated or implied" in the literature available at the time (421).

(a) The ratio of the marginal utilities (the marginal rate of substitution) for each pair of consumers' goods must be the same for all households.

(b) In every industry factors must be combined in a technologically optimum manner.

(c) The marginal value productivity of each factor must be the same in every industry.

(d) In the optimum, there must be no possibility of shifting a worker from one occupation to another to increase the value of output by more than would be required to compensate the worker for the change.

(e) Occupational wage differentials must correspond at one and the same time to differences in marginal value productivity and, for marginal workers, to differences in disutility.

(f) The social dividend or tax, however, must be determined independently of the worker's occupation or earnings. (421–22)

Bergson concludes:

> It is an easy matter to restate the foregoing optimum conditions in terms of "costs." The total cost incurred in the production of the optimum output must be at a minimum and, in the optimum, price must equal marginal cost (since we say nothing about rent, costs may be understood here to comprise material costs, interest, and wages). (424)
>
> The requirement that the total cost of producing the optimum output be a minimum means, of course, that the average cost incurred in the production of this output is a minimum. (424)
>
> [If average cost varies with output (a U-shaped pattern)], marginal and average cost will be equal only at one scale of output, that for which average cost is at a minimum. In the case of indivisibilities, however, the possibility has to be reckoned with also that because of the very heavy overhead and the relatively limited importance of variable costs, average cost per unit will not follow the familiar U-shaped pattern, but instead will continue to decline for a wide range of output variations. Marginal cost may be below average cost for the entire relevant range of operations.
>
> To repeat, however, *the rule for the attainment of the optimum is that price must equal marginal cost.* This principle is perfectly general: it holds regardless of the relation of marginal and average cost, regardless of whether price is above average cost and there are "profits" (as might be so in the case of "fixed factors") or below average cost and there are losses (as might be so also in the case of "fixed factors," and very likely would be so in the case of large indivisibilities).
>
> For this very fundamental proposition, we are indebted chiefly to Marshall and Pigou, who long ago advanced it boldly even for cases of decreasing costs. (425) Of course, . . . in practice what we have to reckon with is not a unique marginal cost for a given level of output, but a complex of marginal costs, each of which is pertinent to a particular period of time. (427)

Bergson anticipated the possibility of adjusting marginal costs to the utility revenue requirement by what is now called the equal percentage of marginal cost rule, as adopted by the California Public Utilities Commission. He considers and votes against that rule. He says:

> The general rule . . . is that price equal marginal cost. What if prices are merely proportional to marginal cost? Would this not suffice? In the face of a good deal of authority for the affirmative, the present writer[42] has argued that the correct answer is in the negative. If prices are proportional but not

equal to marginal costs, the optimum conditions . . . will be violated. In particular, the differences in value productivity of different types of labor will no longer equal differences in wages, and hence will not correspond to differences in disutility. A reallocation of resources, involving the shift in marginal workers from one occupation to another, would be in order.

,42. See A. Bergson, *The Structure of Soviet Wages* (Cambridge, MA: Harvard Univ. Press, 1944), pp. 119–22, which also refers incidentally (p. 21, note 16) to the writings of Lerner and Dickinson on this question. Lerner, who is cited here as having supported the erroneous view that proportionality is sufficient, has *since corrected himself* (*Economics of Control*, p. 100 ff.). (428)

Bergson cites the contribution of Harold Hotelling in his essay. The literature is replete with discussions of Hotelling's famous toll-bridge example, so Hotelling is covered only under *Ruggles*, below.

Comment

While Bergson's language speaks for itself, attention is called to the extreme difficulty of achieving in an *unplanned competitive economy* the interrelated conditions for an optimum allocation cited in his inventory.

Note that Bergson anticipates current microeconomic theory by his statements that for the optimum (a) total cost must be at a minimum, at which point (b) average cost will be at a minimum, so that (c) price equated to marginal cost will also equate to average cost.

However, Bergson is realistic. He recognizes the condition, common for electric and natural gas utilities, of a combination of heavy overhead (or fixed) costs[4] and light variable costs.[5] And he recognizes that under this condition, marginal cost may be below average cost "for the entire relevant range of operations." He would nonetheless set prices at marginal cost, presumably offsetting any losses by a tax subsidy.

Bergson observes that there is not "a unique marginal cost . . . but a complex of marginal costs."

Abba P. Lerner: *The Economics of Control: Principles of Welfare Economics*, 1944

Introduction to Lerner

The central prescription of Abba P. Lerner's[6] *The Economics of Control*[7] is the basic notion of the optimality of marginal cost pricing. As such it introduces much of the theoretic background later utilized (with many refinements) by Alfred E. Kahn in his application of neoclassical microeconomics to the regulated utilities (chapter 4).

It is impossible to condense Lerner's work within the length constraints of this appendix. Indeed, an entire course in graduate-level economics would hardly suffice. Pointed out are only those limited selections from his analysis that, as forerunners of contemporary classical microeconomics, bear most closely upon the marginal cost pricing doctrine.

It is helpful to understand Lerner's context: He sought to outline the measures that a *Ministry of Economic Planning*[8] in a controlled socialist regime would invoke to achieve optimum results for the economy. From this base, he extends his analysis to an uncontrolled capitalist economy, pointing out differences and obstacles that may stand in the way of reaching optimum results in the absence of controls, and particularly to the difficulty of conforming to the requirements of "perfect competition."

The Price-to-Opportunity Cost Link

Central to microeconomics is the link between price and opportunity cost. Lerner's position on this connection between the terms is observed below as an introductory matter.

Lerner distinguishes between "private marginal" and "social marginal" opportunity costs. The former relates to the consumer. It comprises the alternative goods the consumer has to sacrifice to obtain *another unit* of the good in question; it is what the individual privately has to give up in order buy the additional unit. (If meat is 30 cents a pound and fruit is 60 cents a basket [keep in mind that Lerner's prices were vintage 1944], the marginal opportunity cost of anther basket of fruit would be the two pounds of meat.) "The individual reaches the best position available to him when he makes the private marginal opportunity cost of each good equal to its marginal substitutability" (66). Of course, it is essential that the consumer's purchase have no effect on the price.

"Social marginal" opportunity cost relates to society, not to the individual. It is what society has to sacrifice when another unit of any particular good is purchased, namely, the alternative product that might have been produced by the factor that was devoted to the particular good.

Lerner reaches two conclusions: (1) the private marginal opportunity cost and the social marginal opportunity cost are equalized by free consumer purchases in the market; and (2) in this way, each individual is induced, while seeking his own interest, to do that which is in the social interest (66–67).[9]

Because the social marginal opportunity cost of any product is measured by its *price*, the private marginal opportunity cost also is measured by *price*. "This is the essential social utility of the price mechanism" (67).

The Controlled Economic System

The basic Rule (Rule 1), which every manager of production must obey, is this:

> If the value of marginal (physical) product of any factor is greater than the price of the factor, increase output. If it is less, decrease output. If it is equal to the price of the factor continue producing at the same rate. (For then the right output has been reached.) (64)

Lerner adds that the individual manager need have "no knowledge whatever" of values of marginal products anywhere except in his own plant. If all managers follow the rule, "the optimum division of each factor between the production of different goods" will result[10] (64). Lerner contends that "the rule [automatically] equalizes the value of the marginal product of *each* factor in *each* of its uses," because (1) "each manager expands or contracts production until the value of the factor's marginal product is equal to its price," with (2) "the price [being] the same for all managers who purchase the factor" due to the ministry's price controls (65).

Lerner concludes that the rule leads to "the optimum allocation of the factors among the various products" (75).

The Uncontrolled (Capitalist) Economic System

Shifting from a controlled to an uncontrolled (capitalist) economic system, Lerner turns to the theoretic conditions of *perfect competition* in an uncontrolled economy, and finds that *if these conditions are satisfied* the same optimum allocation of resources will result. The conditions are "perfect competition in buying and in selling in every productive unit throughout the whole of an uncontrolled economy" (75), which is geared to a maximization-of-profit principle. He says: "If there is perfect competition throughout the economy individual enterprisers seeking to maximize their profits behave just as if they were following the Rule" (74).

He restates the rule in the context of perfect competition in the uncontrolled economy.

> If the extra revenue from employing another unit of any factor is greater than the increase in cost, increase output (for that will increase the profit). If the fall in revenue from employing a unit less of a factor is less than the fall in cost from so doing, decrease output (for that will increase the profit). If the rise or fall in revenue from changing the quantity of a factor used is equal to the rise or fall in cost, continue producing at the same rate (since the change would not increase the profit). (74)

This restatement employs terms that differ from the rule as given for the controlled economy (Rule 1). The two statements can be brought together by substituting parallel terms into the latter statement.

For	Substitute	Basis
"the rise and fall in cost"	"the price of the factor"	When there is perfect competition in *buying,* the change in *cost* from using more or less of the factor is exactly equal to the price of the factor.
"the rise or fall in revenue"	"the value of the marginal product"	When there is perfect competition in *selling,* the change in *revenue* from varying output by employing more or less of the factor will change the revenues by exactly the value of marginal product.

With these substitutions and with the meaning remaining the same, *the principles for maximizing profit* reads (74–75):

> If the value of the marginal product of any factor is greater than the price of the factor, increase output.
> If the value of the marginal product is less than the price of the factor, decrease output.
> If the value of the marginal product is equal to the price of the factor, continue producing at the same rate.

The above "is identical" to Rule 1 and would lead "in exactly the same way [in an uncontrolled economy] to the optimum allocation of the factors among the various products" (75).

The Welfare Equations

Lerner establishes a basic welfare equation that must be satisfied to reach an optimum condition. This is (76):

$$\text{Marginal Social Benefit} = \text{Marginal Social Cost}$$
$$\text{or}$$
$$msb = msc$$

where the *marginal social benefit* is the net benefit to society from the particular increment of product being considered, and the *marginal social cost* (or *social marginal opportunity cost*) is the sacrifice to society of having the marginal factor used up so that it is not available for use elsewhere; or, expressed differently, it is the alternative social benefit that the marginal factor could have produced if it had been used elsewhere.

This basic final equation is the end result of the chain of subsidiary equations that lead to it. (By reason of the chain, equation one equals equation five). The chain is (76):

1. Marginal Social Benefit (msb) = Value of Marginal Product (vmp) (Requires optimum allocation of consumption goods, and that the buyer is the only individual affected by the purchase)
2. Value of Marginal Product (vmp) = Marginal Private Revenue (mpr) (Requires perfect competition in selling the product)
3. Marginal Private Revenue (mpr) = Marginal Private Cost (mpc) (Requires maximization of profit by producer)
4. Marginal Private Cost (mpc) = Value of Marginal Factor (vmf) (Requires perfect competition in buying factors of production)
5. Value of Marginal Factor (vmf) = Marginal Social Cost (msc) = *Marginal Cost* (mc) = *Price* (p)

The rule may be expressed in terms of marginal cost instead of the marginal quantity of factor. This result is reached by substituting in the equations, (vmp) = (mpr) = (mpc) = (vmf). As commonly used, *marginal revenue* (*mr*) *is* usually substituted for *mpr* (omitting "private" as being understood) and *marginal cost (mc) is* substituted for *mpc* (also omitting "private," for the same reason). Since the rule adjusts output to make *vmp* and *vmf* equal to price (p, the price of the product), the rule may be alternatively stated as $p = mc$ (price = marginal cost), but only under conditions of perfect competition. Absent these conditions, the rule is misleading, although not actually wrong (98–99). [It is pointed out that $p = mc$ is the theoretic underpinning of the marginal cost pricing doctrine which is the subject of chapter 4.]

The Least-Cost Addition to the Rule

Lerner adds "Rule 2" to the primary rule. This requires that production be accomplished *in the cheapest possible way* (130). Rule 2 is an instruction on *how* to produce, which is missing from the first. Its purpose is "to bring about the optimum allocation of the different factors among different production units" (131).

The rule, Lerner points out, "seems good common sense" but is far from simple to implement because of the requirements of the perfect competition model to which it must conform for validity, but for which an unlimited predictive ability on the part of managers would be necessary. Lerner gives this illustration:

> In calculating which was the cheapest way of producing the manager must assume, even if this is not true, that the current prices of the factors are fixed and will not be changed by his own purchases. If this happens to be true everything is all right, but if it is not the matter becomes quite complicated. On the one hand, he must ignore his influence on price in calculating total cost to find that method of production which makes total cost a minimum, but on the other hand he must take it into account because he has to repeat the calculation (ignoring his influence on prices) every time he changes his output or the proportion in which he combines the factors, and if he knew before he made any changes what the effects of those changes would be on the prices he could save himself a great deal of trouble. In any position with given prices his calculations might show that a different method of production was cheaper, yet when the new method was adopted the resultant change in prices might alter the situation so that the old method would appear cheaper (if the new prices were taken as given in the new calculation). The manager would then have to change back to the old method of production or perhaps to some intermediate method. (130)

However, taken together the two rules distinguish between the (1) optimum division of resources in general among different goods, Rule 1, and (2) the optimum allocation of the different factors so as to give the optimum combination of factors in each production unit, Rule 2. That is, Rule 1 tells the producer *how much* to produce of the particular good ($p = mc$, with mc reflecting the value of the alternative product). Rule 2 tells the producer what factors to use, in that the mp of factors is proportional in different uses, so that there is no waste and a resulting optimum allocation of factors among the different production units. Notwithstanding, however, Lerner concludes that "this is a very small thing as the two rules are really interdependent. Neither would be able to guarantee the one optimum unless the other rule were simultaneously bringing about the other optimum" (132). Therefore, Lerner would adopt Rule 1 to "direct the productive forces of society in the best possible way" (132).

Problems of the Perfect Competition Model

Lerner is critical of the widespread adoption of the perfect competition model: Problems arise because of the "excessive attachment of economists to the assumption of perfect competition." Because "the optimum use of resources happens to be one of the consequences of perfect competition" the assumption is made instead of attacking the optimum use directly, thus requiring "elaborate amendments and qualifications in moving from perfect competition to the real world" (131–32).

Lerner singles out the "product indivisibility" requirement of the model for close scrutiny. He finds that "*significant* indivisibility destroys perfect competition" and he reaches the "surprising" conclusion that when increasing returns [decreasing costs] are coupled with pure competition, and an optimum use of resources has been reached ($vmp = pf$, so that profits are at a maximum—or losses at a minimum), it pays the firm to close down! The firm must have "subsidized application of the rule" to avoid running at a loss (176–77).

Public Utilities

Regarding the regulated utilities, Lerner is quoted in full to capture the flavor of his thinking:

> When recognized, indivisibility shows itself in the problem of the public utility, where unintelligent compromise leads to unending regulation.
>
> Industries that are subject to large indivisibilities such as make perfect competition impossible have, by a curious history, come to be called *public utilities*. It has been recognized that perfect competition in these public

utilities cannot be arranged or even permitted and that it would lead to bankruptcy and the cessation of important services to the public. Monopoly is therefore permitted, though public regulation is applied in attempts to limit the degree to which the monopolies depart from the optimum use of resources in their attempts to increase their profits. This compromise between public and private enterprise leads to unending regulations and attempts to evade the regulations and more regulations to stop the evasions. In the tremendous volume of writing on this subject there is confusion which is not entirely unconnected with a natural tendency for the great public utility corporations to try to get the public to identify their unrestricted powers (to sacrifice the optimum use of resources in restricting output and raising prices for the sake of their profits) with the democratic liberties of the citizen. An equally fertile source of confusion is the identification of the elimination of great profit with the optimum use of resources. This identification is brought about by too close a concentration on perfect competition that happens to result in both the absence of great profits and the optimum use of resources. As we have seen, perfect competition cannot be brought about in the circumstances considered, and nothing can be gained by trying to achieve one of its symptoms through legislation aiming at the establishment of another.

In the regulation of public utilities in the United States we have a classical example of how the complexity of regulations in an uncontrolled economy enormously surpasses that needed in a controlled economy. In the controlled economy, public utilities, which by definition cannot be made subject to perfect competition, would be run by public agencies instructed by the Rule to make $vmp = pf$. They would normally be run at a loss, which is justifiable in the name of the optimum use of resources. (181–82)

Is Perfect Competition Possible?

Lerner says "yes," in the absence of indivisibility or where the size of the market is greater than the size of the indivisibility, so that the output of the firm is sufficient to reduce the indivisibility to insignificance. However, while freedom of entry (like government regulation) can prevent excessive profits, it cannot prevent the waste of resources (183).

Average Cost

The predicate for Lerner's reasoning is the same as for the marginal cost pricing doctrine, that is, the equation:

$$p \ (= mr) = mc$$
Price (equals marginal revenue) equals marginal cost

Establishing price at the marginal cost level determines the output of a firm that tries to maximize its profits. *Average* cost (*ac*) plays no part in the analysis. "It does not determine whether the firm shall produce or not or what output it should produce. It merely helps us to calculate whether a firm in production makes enough to cover the fixed cost." Lerner explains:

> The reason for this is that fixed costs are not economically relevant. They have been incurred in the past and they involve no new sacrifice that is involved in present production. They do not form part of the *msc* of production. Only the variable factors represent withdrawals of resources from production elsewhere in order to produce here. Consequently it is natural that the fixed costs should play no part in determining output where the optimum use of resources, equating *msb* to *msc*, *is* brought about by private entrepreneurs under perfect competition. It is for the same reason that it plays no part in the Rule for achieving the same optimum by collectivist agencies. (207)

Relationships of Average Costs to Marginal Costs

Average costs are, however, relevant from a different point of view—their relationships to marginal costs.

Under conditions of *increasing cost* to meet additional demand, *mc* may be higher than *ac*. The reason would be that *mc* rises with the greater output (to pay higher input prices for units of supply) but less than the rise in price. Since *mc is* equated to price, *mc* will be greater than *ac*. The excess of *mc* over *ac is* [economic] rent (a relatively fixed factor contributing an element of surplus), which results under this kind of increasing costs from the competition of entrepreneurs for it. Lerner concludes:

> . . . in these circumstances conditions of pure competition can be maintained, so that it can be said that the absorption of this surplus by the fixed factor plays a socially useful function. It takes away the profits that otherwise might lead to too great an entry into the industry, which would reduce the price below *mc* and so result in a faulty allocation of resources. (225)

Under *decreasing cost*, *mc* (price) falls below *ac* (225). Instead of a surplus, the producer faces a deficit (negative rent). Because no one is willing to absorb this deficit, "the possibility of having an ideal use of resources breaks down unless the state is prepared to absorb this negative surplus by subsidizing the industry. In the absence of such activity by the state, the decreasing cost will lead to monopoly and its deviations from the optimum use of resources" (226).

"An excess of *ac* over *mc* . . . is what makes perfect competition impossible . . . (225) *positive rent or surplus is implied in conditions of perfect competition*" (emphasis added) (226).

Long- versus Short-Period Time Spans

Lerner points out that the value of *mc* in the foundational equation $p = mc$ (with *mc* being appropriately qualified so that it becomes *vmf*) *is* ambiguous in the absence of a specification of the time period to which it applies.

He comments that periods are long or short depending upon the production factors that are considered for adjustment. The longer the period, the greater will be the number of factors (the variable factors) that can be adjusted and the fewer the number of factors (the fixed factors) that cannot. "The longer the period of time taken, the better can be the adjustment to any change in the situation" (212).

He defines a *short* period as one *not long enough* to permit a certain adjustment to be made. A *long* period is any period *that is sufficient* or more than sufficient to permit this adjustment to be made. Thus, the actual period may vary from minutes to a century. The distinction between fixed and variable factors is correspondingly relative.

Lerner advises that "the appropriate period to be used in connection with the Rule is that which refers to *the date of the output considered.*" He explains:

> The marginal cost will be different for increments of output at different dates in the future. The appropriate *mc* to equate to the price of an increment of output at a particular date in the future is that which would be incurred in the course of producing an increment of output at that date. If the expected price at that date is greater than this *mc*, the cost should be incurred and the increment of output produced. If the expected price is less than the appropriate *mc*, the increment of output should not be produced.

Output at that date should rather be reduced until the expected price is once more equal to the appropriate *mc*. If the price is expected to be the same at different future dates, the appropriate adjustments will equalize the different *mc*s. If the prices are expected to be different, different *mc*s are just as appropriate for the increments of output at different dates as for different products becoming available at the same date. (215)

Lerner cautions against the acceptance as true of a common generalization holding that a long-period *mc* will be greater than the short-period *mc* because in the short period only the variable factors are increased, whereas to get the long-period *mc* there must be added the cost of the additional fixed factors that become variable factors in the longer period. This is not necessarily true, he says because, for example, the long-period increase in the factors that are fixed in the short period may permit smaller increases, or perhaps even decreases, in the variable factors that enter into the short-period *mc*. He notes that the contrary could be argued also, although not necessarily true either, namely, that the short-period *mc* can never be less than the long-period *mc*, but may be greater, because if it were less the short-period adjustment would be kept up in the long-period, and the short-period *mc* would *ipso facto* become identical with the long-period *mc*. But this contrary version might be invalidated because of an abnormally low price of the variable factors (resulting in a very low short-period *mc*) which cannot be expected to continue for the long-period adjustment (213).

But, Which Is Better, the Long or Short Period?

Lerner seems equivocal on this question. He says: "If we take a short-period point of view we can consider all manufactured goods as fixed in supply because we do not then have to consider what will happen when the existing supply wears out. That problem belongs to the long period. . . . [The short period] supposes that it exhausts the whole of the future that has to be considered so that there is nothing outside of it, . . . which narrows the horizon so that no possible uses of a factor outside the short period can be seen" (226–27).

On the other hand, "The long-period point of view . . . [has] a horizon that permits one to consider the possibilities of factors being used outside the short period" (229).

Nancy Ruggles: "Recent Developments in the Theory of Marginal Cost Pricing," 1949–1950[11]

Nancy Ruggles gives a comprehensive summary of varying views on the marginal cost pricing doctrine that had been expressed by leading academicians by the middle of the twentieth century. Together with Lerner (above) and Bonbright (below), these provided a theoretic base for Kahn's later *Economics* (1970–71).

As was the case for Lerner, it is not possible to cover Ruggles's work completely. Omitted, for example, are extensive arguments on the type of taxation that might be applied to subsidize the losses to producers that would result from a strict application of the doctrine to decreasing cost industries. Instead, an attempt has been made to outline the matters most closely related to pricing as such, including proportionality; average, marginal, and total costs; increasing or decreasing costs; price discrimination; workability; and the marginal cost conditions.

Ruggles's Statement of the Doctrine

Ruggles sums up the theory in this fashion: "The advocates of marginal cost pricing maintain that in any situation in which all prices are not equal to marginal cost, the general welfare can be increased by setting these prices equal to marginal cost." She adds: "The use of marginal analysis for reaching a [welfare] maximum is, of course, a fundamental part of the methodology of economic analysis" (118).

The Literature

As her subject suggests, Ruggles traces the evolution of the doctrine. She starts with Hotelling's 1938 presentation, which she calls "the credo of those who advocate marginal cost pricing on the grounds of the new welfare economics" (110). Prior to Hotelling, she comments, the "development of the marginal cost pricing principle had for the most part been on a highly theoretical plane concerned with the basic welfare principles, with some attention to the problems of designing an optimum price system for a socialist state" (110) (see Bergson, above).

As a beginning point, Ruggles states that Hotelling "postulated an economy in which products are priced at marginal cost, and the difference between this amount and total cost is made up by taxation" (107).

Deficits requiring such makeup would occur in "decreasing cost industries" (108).

In addition to taxation, revenues for offset could be gained by setting higher prices for "commodities available in limited quantity . . . such as space on trains during holiday periods, prices for which could be set high enough to limit demand to the amount of space available" (108).

Hotelling recognized that "the general wellbeing would have to be purchased at the expense of sacrifices by some . . . who would be expected on balance to suffer a loss" (108–9).

Hotelling's famous toll-bridge example concludes that the marginal cost for use of the bridge is zero. If tolls are charged to make the bridge self-liquidating, usage will be decreased and the total benefit will be reduced (109). He parallels this example by looking at the railroads, where "running costs are only a small fraction of their total costs, and the actual extra costs of marginal use are even smaller. . . . In a rational economic system, rates should be set in such a fashion that they would even out the traffic over the year, ensuring full utilization of capacity at all times. . . . In practice, the exact opposite is true. . ." (109).

Hotelling admitted problems, particularly in interpretation. Ruggles recounts:

> For instance, when a train is completely full the marginal cost of carrying an additional passenger is equal to the cost of running another train, but in the more normal situation when a train is not full the extra cost of carrying an extra passenger is very small. A sharp increase in rates to the unlucky first passenger on each train can be avoided by an averaging of rates according to the probability of having to run another train. If it is not feasible to run another train, a fare should be charged (as was pointed out above) which is of sufficient magnitude to distinguish between the purchasers, enabling those who are willing to pay the most to ride. (109)

Hotelling also recognized the special problem of "expenditures which are not for consumption." Ruggles explains:

> The usual criterion for private investment is whether or not it will pay for itself; but this criterion obviously becomes inapplicable with marginal cost pricing. Hotelling offered instead the criterion that the investment should be undertaken if some distribution of the burden is possible such that everyone concerned would be better off than without the new investment. He stressed that it is not necessary that any such distribution of the

burden be practicable, but did agree that compensation should be paid to those who are injured by the new investment when the failure to compensate would cause undue hardship. (109)

Ruggles credits Hotelling with starting "The Marginal Cost Pricing Controversy." This being economics, there was, of course, both dissension and agreement. Mentioned below are most of the writers included by Ruggles in her review.

R.H. Montgomery (1939) recommended that railroads and electric utilities charge only incremental costs (i.e., price at marginal cost), without attempting to maximize profits. Regnar Frisch (1939) raised the still-present disagreement over "proportionality" (which is evident in the CPUC's equal percentage of marginal costs allocation method). Frisch felt that it was not necessary for prices actually to equal marginal costs provided they were proportional to it, to which Hotelling later agreed. But Lerner (1944) and P.A. Samuelson (1947) disagreed: "exact equality is necessary for consistency in the system as a whole" (111).

J.C. Bonbright, in a 1940 article (before his textbook, below), maintained that "the striking discrepancies between marginal and average costs of public utilities are not due primarily to long-run increasing costs, but rather to the temporary or chronic presence of excess plant capacity, [so that] it is not the difference between long-run and average marginal cost which makes average cost pricing unsatisfactory, but rather the existence of off-peak periods in the short-run" (112).

E.W. Clemens (1941) raised two points, relative to decreasing cost industries: (1) he showed that "since that lowest point on the long-run average cost curve coincides with both the long- and short-run marginal cost curves, only the single criterion of marginal cost is needed, and the condition that average cost be a minimum is superfluous"; and (2) he maintained that marginal cost pricing is *not* the only solution; it is necessary only if a one-price system is postulated. A system of price discrimination [i.e., a block system of rates] could also arrive at the point of ideal output (112).

Ruggles suggests that Lerner (1944, above) "recognized the necessity of meeting all of the marginal conditions, including those of work and leisure—but then, having recognized it, he proceeded to erect a structure which does not meet it . . . [because] the problem of obtaining the desired income distribution [through taxes, etc.] would interfere with satisfying the marginal conditions of work and leisure . . . [a problem] for Lerner, as for other advocates of marginal cost pricing" (114).

Ruggles notes a "practical question concerning the workability of marginal cost pricing" that arises from the disregard of sunk costs. This disregard, pointed out by T. Wilson (1945), overlooks the fact that past experience [a market test] actually *cannot* be ignored in future planning. "A successful enterprise of one type encourages duplication, whereas one that is a failure serves as a warning" (114).

R.H. Coase (1945), while not disagreeing that price should equal marginal cost, "argued that total cost would also have to be covered if there was not to be a redistribution of income in favor of the consumers of products in which fixed costs form a high proportion of total costs . . . [that is], marginal cost pricing without compensation leads to a change in the income distribution, so its result cannot be compared in welfare terms with that of average cost pricing." Coase added that "*correct price discrimination* would permit *both* the marginal and the total conditions to be met" (115). Ruggles continues in observations that are quoted in full because of their direct relevance to the practicalities of pricing:

> Coase further extended his arguments against marginal cost pricing in a later article [1946]. In this article, he developed an example of a situation in which average costs are different from marginal costs, yet all costs are directly assignable to specific consumers. The example is that of purchases from a centrally located store by customers located in a radial pattern, so that delivery to each customer must be made individually. The cost of supplying goods to any customer would then be the store cost of the goods plus the cost of delivery. Together these make up total cost. The charge, he argued, should be a delivery fee plus the store cost of the goods. This device Coase referred to as multi-part pricing. He maintained that Hotelling and Lerner had overlooked this possibility in favor of a system in which all delivery charges would be paid by the public at large through taxation. The adoption of the marginal cost pricing system, he said, would involve a redistribution in favor of those to whom the cost of delivery was greatest—i.e. those who lived farthest away.
>
> *Two fundamental conditions* for an optimum pricing system were laid down in this article. In the first place, Coase said, for each individual consumer the same factor should have the same price wherever it is employed or else the price system will misallocate resources, i.e. the usual marginal conditions of production and exchange must be satisfied. In the second place, Coase said that the period of a factor should be the same for all consumers, since otherwise one consumer would be obtaining more for the same amount of money than another consumer. This is the first instance in which the criterion of *price uniformity* had been held up as a

welfare principle. Coase used it because of his concept of the distribution of income; he stipulated uniform prices to different consumers so that the distribution of money income would be equivalent to the distribution of income in terms of the factors of production. (In no place has he recognized that the question of the utility of the income is also relevant.) But this stipulation of uniform prices is inconsistent with Coase's own earlier statement that correct price discrimination would meet both the marginal and the total conditions. Multi-part pricing, Coase maintained, would satisfy both the marginal conditions and the criterion of uniform factor pricing, and Hotelling and Lerner, by considering only average and marginal cost pricing, omitted the one satisfactory solution.

With respect to the alternative merits of marginal and average cost pricing, Coase emphasized that both systems have advantages and disadvantages. He recognized that if consumers are not allowed to buy additional units at marginal cost there will be a maldistribution of the factors of production, and he also admitted that production which is worth undertaking can sometimes be carried out with marginal cost pricing when it could not with average cost pricing. The disadvantages of marginal cost pricing lie, according to him, in the fact that the income taxes which must be levied to subsidize the decreasing cost industries impose a tax on effort and on waiting, and in the fact that taxing some individuals to provide factors of production for the use of other individuals involves a redistribution of income which cannot be avoided in any way except by levying excise taxes on the products of decreasing cost industries—a self-defeating measure, since it would only result in a return to average cost pricing. With reference to investment, Coase repeated the objections originally raised by Wilson [above] that the *market test* is necessary as a guide, even if it is more conservative than might be wished. Finally, Coase claimed that the marginal cost pricing principle destroys the guide to policy, making it exceedingly easy to make errors. (115–16)

Ruggles cites Melvin Reder (1947) as "one of the most complete discussions of marginal cost pricing, aside from Lerner's," but sees "implicit contradictions" in his work, mainly related to the compensation [taxes] that would be required to make up losses due to marginal cost pricing.

William Vickrey (1948) provided answers to a number of the objections to marginal cost pricing. He advocated this pricing, but, Ruggles comments, "without an examination of the source or nature of the subsidies it would require" (117). Vickrey contended that problems of a marginal cost pricing system arise not because of the system, but because of the existence of *decreasing cost industries* (117). In her Summary and

Evaluation, Ruggles opined that "'discontinuities' and 'inelasticities' [arising because] demand curves are not smooth and continuous and single valued . . . make it possible to meet total costs in many decreasing cost industries without violating the marginal conditions appreciably. . . . Price discrimination between different lines of a product produced by one firm, for instance, is a device to cover total costs by charging more than average cost on some lines and less than average cost on others" (124).

The issue of decreasing cost conditions is mentioned here because they have been predominant in utility history, and they pose special problems in applying the marginal cost pricing doctrine to Information Age industries. Under contra-trend increasing costs conditions, Ruggles believes, the higher marginal costs associated with demand growth can be coupled to the prices for the service primarily giving rise to the growth, such as on-peak air conditioning. Revenue requirements, both historical and future, can be met in this fashion.

Ruggles's Summary and Evaluation

The Questions

Ruggles contends that "the claim for the superiority of marginal cost pricing is based on the argument that it meets the marginal conditions for maximizing welfare, and that for this reason it represents an optimum." An evaluation requires consideration of these questions:

(a) Is meeting these marginal conditions a sufficient basis for recommending a pricing system?
(b) Does the marginal cost pricing system meet these marginal conditions?
(c) Does the marginal cost pricing system, in fact, avoid any necessity for interpersonal comparisons? (118)

Ruggles does not answer her three questions directly, yes or no. Because we cannot quote here in full due to space limitations, it is necessary to attempt (dangerously) to extract the kernels of her thoughts.

Regarding Question (b)

To the extent that prices *are actually* set equal to marginal cost, to that extent it is obvious that marginal cost pricing will meet the marginal conditions.

But . . . the question is not quite so simple. Marginal cost pricing would . . . make necessary the payment of subsidies to producers with decreasing costs, since otherwise they could not cover their total costs.

[This raises the issue of the method of financing subsidies, a complex issue that is passed over here] (118–19).

Regarding Question (c)

The advocates of marginal cost pricing have in general not explicitly discussed the question of interpersonal comparisons—except to the extent of stating that marginal cost pricing would not require them. . . .

Implicit . . . is the idea that it is only necessary that compensation be *possible*, not that it be paid . . . to say that a change to the marginal cost pricing system is desirable.

Certain groups "would probably suffer . . . the general well being would have to be purchased at the cost of sacrifices by some . . . [these sacrifices require] the interpersonal judgment that the loss in utility by those who sacrifice is less than the gain in utility by those who gain . . . .

Arguments in favor of the marginal cost pricing system [are] dependent upon interpersonal comparisons of utility (120–21).

Regarding Question (a)

Ruggles is of the opinion that the marginal cost pricing system rests upon two implicit assumptions: that the marginal utility of income is constant; and that the supply of the factors of production is fixed. The reasonableness of these assumptions "is of prime importance in assessing the practical merits" of the system. She grants that reasonableness is a question of personal opinion. However, her point is that a judgment of the reasonableness of *these* two assumptions *must* be made because the system "does *not* rest upon the [other] assumptions its champions maintain that it does" (122–23).

. . . it is not possible to design a pricing system upon the basis of some criterion of *efficiency*, and then to alter the income distribution system in any desired way without affecting the efficiency of the pricing system. No such separation of the problem is possible. (123)

One of Ruggles's more sweeping conclusions is this: ". . . there are a number of sectors of the economy in which for technological reasons marginal cost pricing would be unsatisfactory," such as distributive firms, retailing, and wholesaling. She continues: "Marginal cost pricing, in other words, does not satisfactorily solve many of the problems which are now disturbing the economy, and there is reason to believe that the adoption of marginal cost pricing might make some of the existing flaws even more troublesome" (124).

She acknowledges, however, that in other sectors "price discrimination which would meet the marginal conditions would not be difficult to arrive at. . . . For example, it is probably true that the use of a block system of rates for electricity does not appreciably interfere with the meeting of the marginal conditions. . ." (124).

The above highly selective excerpts from Ruggles's analysis are concluded by quoting her closing paragraphs in full. These seem to be her final answer to her first question. She concludes:

> Finally, it should be pointed out that there is a whole set of arguments advanced by the advocates of marginal cost pricing which can equally well be used to support pricing at other than marginal cost levels. *Hotelling, for instance, supported the pricing of power projects at marginal cost on the ground that others besides those directly involved would benefit.* This is a very good argument for pricing many commodities below, rather than at, marginal cost. Milk for children, subway transportation in large cities, and many other commodities and services might better be so priced. The nation has a stake in healthy children, and the benefits accrue to others besides the children and those upon whom they are dependent for support. Similarly, it can be argued that the subways benefit landowners, automobile drivers, and employers in large cities. There is therefore no necessary reason why the price charged to those who ride the subways should be equal to marginal cost—some part of that marginal cost might well be borne by the others who benefit from each person's riding, or, if the benefit is widespread, by general taxation.
>
> It thus appears that, since the distribution of income must be taken into account, there is no one general pricing system which will be more efficient than all others for all sectors of economy. *Different pricing principles are economic tools which find applicability in different circumstances. The task of the economist in designing price systems is not so much one of finding a general panacea, but rather one of the systematic analysis of the special problems which arise in different sectors of the economy. Marginal cost pricing may very well increase welfare in certain specific situations. The fact that it is not applicable as a general system does not mean that it should be disregarded altogether. Certain*

railway and utility rates do provide an area in which marginal cost pricing would increase welfare. Hotelling was undoubtedly right in pointing out that the gain enjoyed by those who benefit from the lower price is frequently greater than the loss by those helping to subsidize the industry, and the attempt to assess the burden carefully may lead to greater diseconomy than allocating it incorrectly (even though in so stating he contradicted his original assumptions).

In summary, then, the design of a pricing system must take into account the conditions which do exist in the economy. The various sectors of the economy differ from one another in the restrictions which they impose on the pricing system, and *what is appropriate for one sector may be completely inappropriate for another.* No one formula can be established which will be valid as a general principle. But one statement can be made: the search for a panacea, for a single simple rule by which to guide all conduct, is, because of the technological requirements of the different parts of the economy and because of the problems of redistribution, a vain search and even a foolish one. A set of tools is available with which to accomplish a complicated job. A better job can be done if each tool is used where it is appropriate, instead of throwing away all but one and expecting it to serve all purposes. (125–26)

Concluding Thoughts

Attention is called to certain conclusions of Ruggles, as stated in the above quotation, that diverge from current textbook microeconomics and the later more refined positions of Professor Kahn. Regarding her first paragraph, current thinking is that prices should never be less than marginal (or incremental) costs because if they are less the buyers' payments do not cover the costs of production to society.

Regarding her middle and final paragraphs, microeconomics as now taught suggests that marginal cost pricing should be a model for the entire economy, not just sectors for which it may be considered appropriate.

Regarding her final paragraph, Kahn's *Economics* is tailored specifically to be a specialized guide for pricing under regulation. It is thus "a set of tools" designed to guide regulation toward "economic efficiency" in designing prices. While many of the precepts of the *Economics* are equally applicable to other economic sectors, that is not the purpose of Kahn's work.

In general, though, Ruggles challenges some of the underlying principles of contemporary microeconomics. She thus presents a broad framework for analysis of opposing theories.

James C. Bonbright: *Principles of Public Utility Rates*, 1961

Here are addressed the views on marginal costs of one of the great utility economists, James C. Bonbright of Columbia University, as presented in his text dated October 10, 1960.[12] The sections referred to below are, in Bonbright's own words, a "critique" of marginal costs as a pricing doctrine from the viewpoint of the myriad considerations that should enter into utility rates.

Short-Run versus Long-Run Marginal Costs

"'Marginal cost' (MC) is a highly ambiguous term" (318). "In its general sense . . . it refers to the increase in total cost of production imposed by a relatively small ('marginal') increase in rate of output. Usually this increase is expressed in terms of an incremental cost per unit of increased output" (318–19).

Short-run or short-term MCs are "estimated under the assumption that the enhanced rate of output will be *temporary* and will hence be accomplished solely by an increase in the rate of utilization of the existing plant and equipment" (319).

Herein lies a "vital distinction" . . . between *constant* costs and *variable* costs (320). Capital costs are treated as a constant and are excluded. So is a large share of operating expenses, including annual depreciation, because these expenses may not vary (at least not materially) with changes in the rate of plant utilization (320). These exclusions from total costs often result in short-run marginal costs (SRMC) being "mere fractions of average total costs" (320). The SRMC of a hydroelectric plant "with redundant capacity and with no opportunity to store water for future use . . . may be practically zero" (320).

Bonbright notes that the term "out-of-pocket cost" may be equated to marginal cost, but if used to reflect only additional *cash* outlays it is not an equivalent because marginal cost should also include noncash costs (such as higher depreciation due to wear and tear) attributable to an increase in output (317, n. 2). Bonbright seems to use the terms "marginal costs" and "incremental costs" synonymously, whether speaking of the short or long run.

Long-run or long-term MCs are "estimated under the assumption that the enhancement in rate of output will *continue indefinitely* and hence will be accomplished by an appropriate increase in adaptation of plant capacity" (319). The increase in the rate of output must be assumed to be sustained long enough to support a change in the capacity and design of the plant and equipment, so that capital and operating costs (which are excluded as a constant in the short-run analysis) become variable (324).

However, it is not strictly necessary that the long-run cost analysis assume all costs, including all capital costs, to be variable. Except in the very long run, some important elements of costs (such as rights-of-way) may remain "almost unaffected" by changes in output, and therefore may be regarded as remaining constant (326).

Bonbright reminds us that changes in outputs may vary with the measure of the change: in demand, in volumetric throughput, or in number of customers (328).

Bonbright also calls attention to situations where the distinction between long and short run is mixed, such as on-peak as contrasted to off-peak service. His view is that for permanently off-peak service, only short-run analysis is applicable: "No component of plant capacity cost or capital costs should be included in the estimate of marginal cost." In contrast, the long-term marginal costs of peak service should "include full allowances for whatever increments in capacity costs may be warranted in order to add to the supply of this type of service" (329). The two services might be regarded as joint-products, with the off-peak service as the by-product (329).

Bonbright recognizes that utility investments may be "lumpy" (he says "jumpy") due to the provision of temporary excess capacity as major plant additions are made. Here the problem of long-run marginal cost determination is not easy: "One must attempt some estimate of average incremental costs per unit of output over the life of the indivisible asset. *This possible solution is fraught with difficulties.* But so, for that matter, is the solution of any problem of long-run utility cost imputation" (331).

The Philosophy of Marginal Cost Pricing

Chapter XX is entitled "The Philosophy of Marginal-Cost Pricing." First Bonbright points out the dichotomy between two principles of utility rates: that rates as a whole should cover total costs, on the one hand, while specific rates should be based on the costs of specific amounts and types of service, on the other. The two goals "are incompatible except under a somewhat rare coincidence" (386).

Some economists say "let rates be set at marginal costs," with any revenue deficiency being met by a tax-financed subsidy, or any revenue excess recaptured through taxation. "What these economists here propose is a narrowing of the role of public utility rates as instruments of economic control . . . that rates should be called upon to perform only those functions which they will perform when designed as if their sole purpose were to control the effective demand for the services." "More thorough-going marginalists," he adds, are concerned with using rates "to secure the optimum utilization of an existing utility plant . . . and would apply a short-run measure of marginal costs—a measure which may seriously detract from the usefulness of rates in the determination of the demand for and the supply of utility services over extended periods of time" (387–88).

On "the underlying idea," Bonbright summarizes:

> Under perfect competition . . . the prices of all products "tend" to come into equality with their average unit costs of production, in that such an equality is one of the conditions of static equilibrium. But these prices also "tend" to equal marginal costs, both of short-run and of long-run varieties. There is no inconsistency among these multiple conditions of equilibrium as long as the products in question are produced at unit costs that either stay constant despite a change in the rates of output, or else increase with increases in output. But if any product should be produced under a condition of *decreasing* unit costs, the maintenance of perfect competition is impossible.
>
> Public utilities belong to a group of industries that are supposed to operate under the latter condition, at least in the typical case—a fact often cited as accounting for the need for their regulation as a substitute for competition. But the very condition which rules out actual competition also rules out any attempt to secure by regulation *all* of the good attributes of competitive prices including those of an equilibrium position in which prices are simultaneously equal to a whole variety of costs including average total costs, short-run marginal costs, and long-run marginal costs. (388–89)

Bonbright then recites the familiar toll-bridge example of Hotelling.

Short-Run Marginal Cost Rate Making

The argument in favor "is implicit in the . . . acceptance of 'out-of-pocket cost,' the popular version of marginal cost, as a measure of minimum rates" (391). In a more academic tone, the argument for adopting short-run marginal costs as a basis for minimum rates is "the proposition that the costs which should govern the rates to be charged at any given time are the costs that actually prevail at this time and not the costs that will or would prevail on the average during an indefinite period in the future. These current costs are governed by the relationship between the present output of service and the present capacity of the plant." If there is overcapacity, rates should be lowered; if there is inadequate capacity, they should be raised (331–32). But such changes in rates reflecting short-run marginal costs are "highly volatile," and may not give consumers the insight to make more rational longer-term decisions (334; also see 333, n. 13).

In his "critique" of proposals to fix rates at short-run marginal costs, Bonbright makes five points. First, he says that, "with most public utilities, the really significant choice is not a simple choice between marginal cost and average cost as a basis of ratemaking. . . . [Most rate structures can be materially improved] without abandoning the total-cost principle. While [improvements] cannot be expected to have all of the consumer-rationing advantages of unqualified marginal cost pricing, neither can they be assumed to result in economic losses of the order of magnitude of those suggested by an attempt to make a particular bridge toll financially self-sufficient. . . . Unfortunately, however, the measures of the relative gains and *losses of marginal cost pricing versus any given type of discriminatory full-cost pricing that are suggested by economic theory are impossible to apply in terms of present factual knowledge*" (395–96). "Secondly," he says, "we must consider whether or not the almost undeniably superior efficiency of short-run marginal-cost pricing *as a means of securing the optimum utilization of a plant of temporarily redundant capacity*[12] warrants the surrender or impairment of all of the other important functions of utility rates, even the function of aiding in the control of the demand for and supply of utility services in the longer run," adding in a footnote:

---

12. Even this claim of superiority must be conceded only on the assumption that the better-than-nothing use of temporarily excess capacity will not materially interfere with possible emergency use. Instant readiness to serve may well be the best use of idle capacity." (396)

"Thirdly, there is the probability that short-run marginal-cost rate making would deprive utility managements of an almost essential guide to intelligent decisions as to the needs for plant expansion. If current rates were to rise and fall with changes in current marginal costs, the resulting unpredictability of future demands might seriously handicap managements in timing their programs of construction" (397).

The fourth and fifth points of Bonbright's critique relate to taxation, the fourth posing the question of "whether the claimed advantages of short-run marginal-cost pricing as a means of improving utility rate structures, even if substantial, would still be great enough to warrant the required resort to tax-financed subsidies" (398). The fifth point relates to the type of tax that might be selected (399).

Bonbright concludes:

> One may summarize the foregoing criticisms of the proposal to base utility rates on short-run marginal costs by saying that, in giving sole consideration to one very limited though important function of prices, that of securing the optimum utilization of whatever plant capacity exists at a particular time, it would surrender other functions of even greater importance including, particularly, that of the long-run control of the demand for and supply of utility services. (399–400)

The Alternative Standard of Long-Run Marginal Costs

Bonbright says:

> Advocates of either [short-run or long-run marginal] cost as a measure of reasonable rates accept, as the primary objective of ratemaking policy, an optimum-allocation or consumer-rationing objective even if its realization calls for the surrender of the traditional principle of financial self-sufficiency. But the long-run marginalists emphasize the need for a relatively stable and continuous level or trend of rates, in the belief that the rates which have the most important effects on the demand for and provisions for utility services are rates that may be expected to persist over a considerable period of time. Hence, the most important marginal costs for purposes of rate control are the normal or persistent marginal costs rather than the very short-lived marginal costs that may fall almost to zero in some brief period of time, only to rise to several times average total costs soon thereafter. For this purpose, however, "long-run" marginal costs must be given a flexible and frankly indefinite interpretation, since any attempt to fix rates today by reference to cost functions that may not materialize, say, for twenty-five years or more would be utterly foolish. In short, the costs that should be covered by the rates are the

marginal costs that are "permanent" in the sense used by a dentist when he refers, optimistically, to a permanent rather than a temporary filling.

Although long-run marginal-cost rate making must rest its claim for acceptance primarily on its asserted superiority from the standpoint of optimum resource allocation, it has an important secondary advantage over the short-run alternative in requiring far less drastic departures from the orthodox requirement of full-cost pricing. . . .

The very reasons, however, which make the proposal to set utility rates at long-run marginal costs more "practical" than the proposal to adjust rates to short-run changes in marginal costs also constitute reasons for doubting its net advantages over full-cost pricing as a generally applicable basis of rate control. Its best claim for serious consideration can be made in those situations in which the traditional attempt to make "rates as a whole cover costs as a whole" must be judged hopeless or intolerably wasteful in the light of experience. (400–402)

Bonbright adds, in a footnote mentioning a 1955 article by Robert W. Harbeson: "Harbeson comments on one criticism not discussed in this brief chapter: that the supporters of marginal-cost pricing for regulated monopolies ignore the supposed failure of unregulated prices to come into accord with marginal costs under the most widely prevailing types of competition, namely, "imperfect" or "monopolistic" competition (395, n. 11).

The Public Interest and "Welfare Economics"

Bonbright has this to say under the above heading at an early point in his book. Quoting in full:

No chapter on "the public interest" or on "maximum social welfare" as the ultimate objective of rate-making policy can afford completely to ignore a restricted conception of economic welfare developed by that modern branch of economics called "theoretical welfare economics" or (quite illegitimately) simply "welfare economics." In line with Western European tradition, this school of thought identifies the welfare of any given community with the totality of the welfares of the individuals therein. Also in line with this tradition, it accepts the revealed choices or preferences of individuals as determining the relative satisfactions derivable by these individuals from alternative forms of action. This acceptance of the preferred position as the position more conducive to individual welfare is what gave specious support to the contention, now no longer advanced, that welfare economics can pass judgment on economic welfare without taking any position on ethical values.

Up to this point there is nothing esoteric in the welfare economist's conception of economic welfare. What is esoteric, however, is his denial of any scientific basis by which one may make interpersonal welfare comparisons—by which one may decide whether an economic change that adds to the welfare of some individuals while detracting from the welfare of others will enhance or diminish net social welfare. This self-denial limits the welfare economists (of the more rigorous persuasion) to attempt to pass judgment on the welfare implications of those proposed changes in economic policy which, while benefiting some members of the community, will not be adverse to any other members. Needless to say, such a limitation is a serious impediment to the resolution of controversies in the field of public utility rate making, since most of these controversies present a clash of interests among the parties to the dispute. And only to a minor extent is the impediment removed by the qualification, now generally accepted in welfare economics, that any proposed economic change will contribute to total economic welfare if the individual beneficiaries, after being actually made to indemnify all the individual losers, will still remain net beneficiaries.

For the reason just suggested, as well as because of the variety of oversimplified assumptions on which reliance must be placed to prove the validity of propositions as to what action will tend to enhance economic welfare, theoretical welfare economics has only a limited usefulness to persons concerned with practical problems of rate making or rate regulation. But "limited usefulness" by no means implies trivial usefulness. On the contrary, a study of the norms of "optimum pricing" set forth by modern welfare economists should help materially in the development of practical principles of rate making. This statement applies notably to the analysis of marginal-cost pricing in the American and European literature of welfare economics—a subject to be discussed in Chapter XX [reviewed above]. (39–41; footnotes omitted)

Comment

Like Bergson, Lerner, and Ruggles, Bonbright speaks for himself. Attention is called here only to points that may deserve special emphasis.

Bonbright declares: "'Marginal cost' is a highly ambiguous term." This is a crucial observation. Microeconomic theory and the "marginal cost pricing doctrine" tilt with this ambiguity, much as Don Quixote tilted with his windmills.

To the theorist, Bonbright's comment that the term "*theoretical* welfare economics" is "quite illegitimately" shortened to "welfare economics" poses an interesting subject for debate.

Finally, Bonbright foresees an important line of reasoning that is not pursued here. He points to "the variety of *oversimplified assumptions* on which *reliance must be placed* to prove the validity of propositions [that marginal cost pricing] will tend to enhance economic welfare . . ." (emphasis added). Herein, reliance is placed on Professor Kahn's exposition of the doctrine, and its applicability to regulated utility pricing, as summarized in chapter 4. Like the writers whose views have been abstracted in this appendix, Kahn speaks for himself.

It would be most instructive—and fabulously interesting—if Bonbright were still alive today and could give his conclusions on attempts to translate marginal cost theory into actual regulated prices.

Notes

Introduction

1. Lawrence H. Summers, Secretary of the Treasury, "The New Wealth of Nations," remarks to Hambrecht & Quist Technology Conference, San Francisco, CA, May 10, 2000.

2. The *MIT Dictionary of Modern Economics*, 4th ed., ed. David W. Pearce (Cambridge, MA: MIT Press, 1992) says:

> *[N]ormative economics.* Economic analysis which provides prescriptions or statements about "what should be" rather than what "is." Normative economics gives rise to statements such as "monopolies should be regulated" or "profits should be taxed."
>
> This type of economics may be contrasted with *positive* economics, which is concerned with describing and analyzing the economy as it is. In effect, normative economics is constructed from positive economics and some judgments about what society's objectives should be (also known as *value judgment*). Thus we may dispute a statement of normative economics either because we consider the positive analysis to be incorrect or because we disagree with the value judgments involved. (310)

Chapter 1. The Challenge to Orthodoxy

1. Lawrence H. Summers, Secretary of the Treasury, "The New Wealth of Nations," remarks to Hambrecht & Quist Technology Conference, San Francisco, CA, May 10, 2000.

2. J. Bradford DeLong, professor, University of California at Berkeley, and Lawrence H. Summers, president, Harvard University, "The 'New Economy': Background, Historical Perspective, Questions, and Speculations," presented at the symposium on Economic Policy for the Information Economy of the Federal Reserve Bank of Kansas City, Jackson Hole, Wyoming, August 30–September 1, 2001, as printed in the proceedings of the symposium.

3. For interesting comments on this question, see Martin Neil Baily and Robert Z. Lawrence, "Do We Have a New E-conomy," *American Economic Review* 91, no. 2 (May 2001): 308–12. On a related matter, see Paul Gompers and Josh Lerner, "The Venture Capital Revolution," *Journal of Economic Perspectives* 15, no. 2 (Spring 2001): 145–68.

4. Summers's reference to "Smithian" calls attention to the legacy of Adam Smith's "invisible hand" analogy in the economic literature, found in his *Inquiry into the Nature and Causes of the Wealth of Nations* (1776). This title often is cited simply as *The Wealth of Nations.* The title of Summers's June 2000 speech, "The New Wealth of Nations," springs from Smith's title, contrasting the economies of 2000 with those of 1776.

5. Summers's "Schumpeterian" refers to Joseph A. Schumpeter (1883–1950), who emphasized the leading role played by entrepreneurs in innovating new products, new techniques, new markets, and new organizational methods.

6. Summers does not mention "natural" monopolies, where price regulation is substituted for competition. These are not mentioned in the antitrust statutes either, which are both broad and vague. However, many courts and commentators have treated the existence of a natural monopoly as a defense against a monopolization charge.

7. Summers uses the term "monopoly power." This power is the ability of a firm (or group of firms) to influence or set the market price.

8. As will be explained later, prices set at SRMC are considered to be the ideal by welfare/normative economics, resulting in "economic efficiency."

9. A more precise definition is that these out-of-pocket costs are the additional expenditures required to raise output from one level to another *within the capacity of preexisting plant facilities and/or preexisting knowledge.* In other words, plant or knowledge need not be improved to expand output. They are static.

10. Alan Murray, "For Policy Makers, Microsoft Suggests Need to Recast Models—Agencies Scramble as Web Poses Good Monopolies, Skews Classic Economics," *Wall Street Journal,* June 9, 2000.

11. Many economists contend that sunk costs, having been incurred *in the past,* are irrelevant to pricing *for the future.*

Chapter 2. Reflections on the Summers Thesis

1. There is room to quibble a bit with this. Because SRMC includes no overage beyond bare out-of-pocket outlays, the producer has no price incentive to continue output at an SRMC price and could discontinue production as easily as continue it. Of course, there may be nonprice motivations to continue production. Lacking such motivations, however, there should be some overage, however small, to induce continued production.

2. Robert M. Solow, *Monopolistic Competition and Macroeconomic Theory* (Cambridge, MA: Cambridge University Press, 1998). Reviewed by N. Gregory Mankiw, Harvard University, *Journal of Economic Literature* (June 2000).

3. This statement does not depend upon any particular definition of marginal cost. It is solely arithmetic. Presumably, the initial monopolistic price covers (a) the marginal (or variable) costs of producing an extra unit *plus* (b) the costs of the existing investments made to have in place and operative the capacity in plant or

knowledge necessary to produce the extra unit (capital costs) *plus* (c) an extra increment of profit above normal capital costs made possible by the assumed monopoly
power. *C* disappears by definition if monopoly power is eliminated. Any reduction
in *A* and *B* in the price offered by competitors erodes full recovery by the monopolist
of *A* and *B*. Of course, all price competition poses this threat of erosion. The New
Economy is not unique in this respect.

4. Faced with a shortage of skilled talent, many employers are offering perks
such as child-care centers, home offices, concierge services, and commuting subsidies, as well as establishing satellite offices to reduce employees' travel time. A few,
notably in high-cost housing areas, are also offering housing subsidies for lower-
paid professionals in short supply, such as teachers.

5. Previously, out-of-pocket expenditures for exceptional talent have been kept
relatively low by offering stock ownership in the new innovative firm as a substitute
incentive. But the allure of stock ownership has been weakened as failures of new
firms have become more frequent, and their stock appreciation more uncertain. So
the future may necessitate higher cash expenditures for sought-after employees than
heretofore.

6. This generality disregards recycling possibilities. Both may be recycled. Oil
used for lubrication (but not when used for fuel) can be refined again and reused.
Metals from a demolished construction project can be reclaimed and applied to a
new project. But recycling itself requires use of scarce resources.

7. Patents do not seem to be as useful for the protection of computer software.
The intricacies of new software are hard to keep within house and it is harder still to
prevent competitors from launching an improvement as "new" to be marketed under
their own label.

8. Gardiner Harris, "New Script—Drug Firms Stymied in the Lab, Become
Marketing Machines," *Wall Street Journal,* July 6, 2000.

9. Heather Green, Norm Alaster, and Timothy J. Mallaney, "Commentary: Guess
What—Venture Capitalist Aren't Geniuses," *Business Week,* July 10, 2000, p. 44.

10. Here comes to mind a comment by an authority whose identity I cannot
recall. The comment was that economics is the only science where two people can
receive Nobel prizes for exactly the opposite conclusions.

11. Short-run and long-run distinctions are important here. Short-run marginal
cost excludes profit, which is not incremental to a change in output. However, in the
long run, firms surviving competition will price at their minimum average cost of
production, which includes fixed costs and normal profits.

Chapter 3. Marginal Costs and Marginalism: Background and Application

1. For an insightful historical and current review of cost-benefit ratios, see Joseph Persky, "Cost-Benefit Analysis and the Classical Creed," *Journal of Economic
Perspectives* 15, no. 4 (Fall 2001): 199–208. Persky says: "Cost-benefit analysis
provides the dominant economic approach with which economists talk to each other,
to government bureaucrats and to the general laity about the desirability of public
programs and investment projects. Cost-benefit studies have pushed economic thinking into public debates. . . ." (199). He adds: ". . . the history (of cost-benefit analysis)

reflects unresolved debates over the appropriate normative foundations for welfare economics" (200). Among these unresolved questions is the academic problem of interpersonal comparisons of utility.

2. F.M. Scherer discusses "the state of economic thought" as related to "the average total cost function and its relationship to marginal and fixed costs" in his article "An Early Application of the Average Total Cost Concept," *Journal of Economic Literature* 39, no. 3 (September 2001): 876–901.

3. This book does not take a side either for or against the theory. The theory is accepted as a given. Numerous advocates have propounded its virtues. Numerous dissenters have criticized its shortcomings. The pros and cons are of immense importance to microeconomics, but only those that bear upon the Summers statement are mentioned.

Chapter 4. Achieving Economic Efficiency in Regulated Pricing as Framed by Alfred E. Kahn

1. Alfred E. Kahn, *The Economics of Regulation: Principles and Institutions: Principles*, Vol. 1 (New York, London, Sydney, Toronto: John Wiley, 1970), and *The Economics of Regulation: Principles and Institutions: Institutional Issues*, Vol. 2 (1971). Mostly, quotations are from Volume 1: for this reason only page numbers are cited. The page numbers of the few quotations from Volume 2 are cited as "II, __." Headings and emphasis not in the printed text have been added in some instances.

2. Alan L. Madian, writing in the January/February 1997 issue of the *Electricity Journal*, distinguishes between static and dynamic efficiency. He says:

> Static efficiency focuses on the short term, defined as the period during which resources are fairly immobile. Static efficiency requires production and distribution by those with the lowest costs. In supplying electric power, both economic dispatch and economy sales can achieve static efficiency . . .
>
> Dynamic efficiency focuses on the longer term during which resources will transfer between sectors depending on anticipated returns. For dynamic efficiency investment decisions are the dominant issue. Economic efficiency that allows for significant investment is dynamic.
>
> Dynamic efficiency is achieved when the total resource costs of the prospective productive facilities, both investment costs and operating costs, are less than the operating costs of the supplanted productive facilities. Dynamically efficient investments achieve resource savings for the society as a whole, though benefits are likely to be unevenly distributed with some left with obsolete facilities.

3. Lerner (Appendix, Pre–Kahn Theory) calls attention to a common misconception that short-run marginal costs will always be less than long-run ones, which he says may not necessarily hold in all cases. This article points out such an exception. Because of the "enormous increase" in the price of oil that had occurred, the "extremely high variable costs of operating existing oil-fired generating capacity" placed short-run costs "far above" long-run costs.

4. Many commissions use "LRMC," substituting "marginal" for "incremental." Kahn often uses the terms interchangeably.

5. Page numbers appearing after quotations in this section are from *American Economic Review* 69, no. 2. The lecture was published in part in *Regulation* (November/December 1978). The American Economic Association printed the lecture in full.

6. Because of Kahn's Civil Aeronautics Board position at the time, the bulk of his lecture concerns the airlines industry. Herein are abstracted in the main only those quotes having direct bearing on marginal cost pricing for electricity and natural gas.

7. Alfred E. Kahn and William B. Shew, "Current Issues in Telecommunications Regulation: Pricing," *Yale Journal on Regulation* (Spring 1987): 194–254.

8. Joint costs are incurred only for joint products that can be produced only in fixed or unvarying proportions. Common costs arise from products that are produced in common in proportions that can be varied. Common costs are pervasive in public utilities.

9. Page numbers designate the pagination of the October 1994 and April 1998 issues of *Electricity Journal* in which these articles were published.

10. Alfred E. Kahn, *Letting Go: Deregulating the Process of Deregulation* (East Lansing: Institute of Public Utilities, Michigan State University, Public Utilities Papers, 1998). Cited page numbers refer to this edition.

11. These are not extensions of the marginal-cost pricing doctrine, and should not be read as such.

Chapter 6. Special Cases: Mixed Issues/ Mixed Methodologies

1. In his May 10, 2000 paper, Summers commented: "An information-based world is one in which more of the goods that are produced will have the character of pharmaceuticals or books or records, in that they involve large fixed costs and much smaller marginal costs." Later he added: ". . . the most important innovations that we see today are built on progress in basic science . . . a crucial component of public policy at this time must be strong support for basic research."

2. Because of the difficulty in distinguishing between basic and applied research, and between research and development, the term "R&D" in this chapter refers primarily to research for any purpose, and makes no attempt to draw a line between where research ends and development begins. Both activities, however, precede manufacturing.

3. There may be notable exceptions to this generality. Production problems for flu vaccine led to a severe shortage in the fall of 2000, when distribution usually is begun. The shortage was so severe that the vaccine was unavailable even to many people who were more vulnerable.

Because formulas for the vaccine differ from year to year, production is not standardized, which differs from the production of aspirin. This lack of uniformity suggests higher costs.

The 2000 experience seemed to reveal flaws in the vaccine distribution process as well as its production. For some unexplained reason, a number of retailers had supplies of the vaccine for sale in their stores at the same time that hospitals and doctors' offices were without. The suggested reason is that these merchants put in their orders early, and thus beat out the normal purchasers.

4. The difficulties involved in such studies are recognized. While the approach itself is straightforward, the cost and output variables are inherently judgmental. Assuming adversarial proceedings, each variable is likely to be hotly contested.

Judge Bork might contend that evaluation of the relative efficiencies in the comparative scenarios is impossible. It is agreed that a *precise* evaluation might be as elusive as a search for the Holy Grail. However, an *indicative* evaluation might be useful as a signal pointing in the right direction for the antitrust effort.

5. Robert H. Bork, *The Antitrust Paradox: A Policy at War with Itself* (New York: Basic Books, 1978).

6. Ibid.

Chapter 7. Antitrust

1. Agriculture is often suggested as an industry that comes closest to perfect competition.

2. In the long run, equilibrium will be reached when the price equals long-run *average* cost, not long-run *marginal* cost as in the case of perfect competition.

3. *Nonsuspect prices:* It is perhaps redundant to point out that our free-market society accepts as valid the overwhelming bulk of prices that prevail throughout the economy. Perfect competition is not a prerequisite for valid prices, which on the whole are established under conditions of less than perfect competition. The suggestion for a cost evaluation is directed only to prices that are suspect because they have been challenged as possibly being in violation of the antitrust statutes. Further, it is pointed out that antitrust adjudications may focus on elements other than price, such as presumed monopolistic practices of the seller (as seems to be the thrust of the government's position in the Microsoft case). This chapter omits any evaluation of monopolistic practices except as they may be revealed by cost analyses.

4. Robert H. Bork, *The Antitrust Paradox: A Policy at War with Itself* (New York: Basic Books, 1978).

5. Bork recognizes that some Supreme Court decisions have interpreted the statutes as having different goals, primarily the survival or comfort of small business, that is, small business welfare, as contrasted with consumer welfare.

6. Bork explains: "Business efficiency necessarily benefits consumers by lowering the costs of goods and services or by increasing the value of the product or service offered" (7).

7. For simplicity, this is illustrated by adopting a single per-unit amount, recognizing that "a price" may actually be a composite package of complex terms and conditions.

8. Note that "innovation" is a simplified term. Its parallel is "price discrimination." The latter term is better expressed as "unreasonable" price discrimination, for some discrimination is unavoidable and reasonable (e.g., the grouping of utility customers into classes with a uniform price for all customers in the class, although the costs to serve individual customers within the class may vary widely). It seems that there may be comparable distinctions for innovation, where some advances are simply minor improvements to be disregarded, while others are substantive. Thus, the simple term innovation might have to be construed as "significant" innovation.

9. Michael J. Mandel, Mike France, and Dan Carney, "The Great Antitrust Debate," *Business Week*, June 26, 2000.

10. There are some circumstances where antitrust law is already doing this. For example, in tying cases under the Clayton Act, some courts, when deciding whether the tying and tied products are "separate" products, consider whether the two products work better in combination, and if so, exclude such a combination from the act.

Appendix

1. At the time, Abram Bergson was associate professor of economics at the University of California, Berkeley.

2. This essay is a part of the American Economic Association's volume *A Survey of Contemporary Economics*, ed. Howard S. Ellis (Blakiston, 1948). Page citations refer to the volume as reprinted in 1949.

3. Bergson might have said, just as accurately: "socialist/welfare/normative economics."

4. In the main text this condition is referred to as one of decreasing unit costs for the range of outputs capable of being produced by an existing plant structure in a capital-intensive industry.

5. Light variable costs, in conjunction with heavy fixed costs, suggest a "surplus capacity" condition.

6. At the time, Lerner was associate professor on the Graduate Faculty of the New York School for Social Research.

7. Abba P. Lerner, *The Economics of Control* (New York: Macmillan, 1944). Page citations in this section refer to this work.

8. Bergson describes the ministry as a *Central Planning Board.*

9. Lerner cautions: "We may repeat that these calculations are applied to the margin. We do not consider what else could have been produced if the whole production of a particular good were given up, or even a very large block of it, but how much more of another product could have been produced if one unit of factor were shifted from this to the alternative product" (67).

10. Lerner makes this contrast: "It is by promulgation and maintaining the general rules consciously directed toward the optimum operation of the whole economy that the *controlled economy* is distinguishable from the *uncontrolled economy* which does not so establish the general rules. The uncontrolled economy will indeed generally show a much more luxurious and complex growth of *particular* regulations. These naturally arise from attempts to correct particular failures resulting from the absence of any general plan for the economy as a whole" (64–65).

11. Nancy Ruggles, "Recent Developments in the Theory of Marginal Cost Pricing," *Review of Economic Studies* 17, no. 2 (1950): 107–26. Page numbers as cited refer to this volume.

12. James C. Bonbright, *Principles of Public Utility Rates* (New York: Columbia University Press, 1961). This is Bonbright's original text of which he is the sole author, and upon which much of his enormous reputation rests. This edition is to be distinguished from the second edition, published in March 1988, with the same title. The second edition, published after Bonbright's death in 1985, was co-authored with Albert L. Danielsen and David R. Kamerschen. This later edition was published by Public Utilities Reports, Inc. Page citations refer to the 1961 edition.

Index

About the Author

Roger Conkling brings to this book a lifetime of experience in governmental and corporate policy making. He has been a federal executive, a nationally known consultant, a senior officer of a utility company, and now—since retirement—he is on the faculty of the University of Portland.